the
witness

the witness

by

KENNETH A. KUNTZ

**saying
yes
when life
says no**

**CBP Press
St. Louis, Missouri**

Scripture passages are taken from the Revised Standard Version of the Bible, copyrighted 1946, 1952, ©1971, 1973 by the Division of Christian Education of the National Council of Churches of Christ in America.

The Garden of the Prophet by Kahlil Gibran. Copyright 1933 by Kahlil Gibran and renewed 1961 by Mary G. Gibran. Reprinted by permission of Alfred A. Knopf Inc.

From *The Unicorn and Other Poems* by Anne Morrow Lindbergh. Copyright © 1956 by Anne Morrow Lindbergh. Reprinted by permission of Pantheon Books, a Division of Random House Inc.

From *The Poetry of Robert Frost* edited by Edward Connery Lathem. Copyright 1942 by Robert Frost. Copyright © 1969 by Holt, Rinehart and Winston. Copyright © 1970 by Lesley Frost Ballantine. Reprinted by permission of Henry Holt and Company, Inc.

Reprinted by permission of The Putnam Publishing Group from *The White Cliffs* by Alice Duer Miller. Copyright © 1940, 1968 Renewed. All Rights Reserved.

Library of Congress Cataloging-in-Publication Data
Kuntz, Kenneth A.
    The witness : saying yes when life says no / Kenneth A. Kuntz.
        p.   cm.
    Includes bibliographical references.
    ISBN 0-8272-4228-X
    1. Meditations. 2. Prayers. 3. Consolation. I. Title.
    BV4832.2.K83   1990
    242--dc20   90-35089
                                                          CIP

Printed in the United States of America

Hold High the Torch!

Hold high the torch!
You did not light its glow—
'Twas given you by other hands, you know.
'Tis yours to keep it burning bright,
Yours to pass on when you no more need light;
For there are other feet that we must guide,
And other forms go marching by our side;
Their eyes are watching every smile and tear
And efforts which we think are not worthwhile,
And sometimes just the very helps they need,
Actions to which their souls would give most heed;
So that in turn they'll hold it high
And say, "I watched someone else carry it this way."
If brighter paths should beckon you to choose,
Would your small gain compare with all you'd lose?
Hold high the torch!
You did not light its glow—
'Twas given you by other hands, you know.
I think it started down its pathway bright,
The day the Maker said: "Let there be light."
And He once said, who hung on Calvary's tree—
"Ye are the light of the world." . . . Go! . . . Shine—for me.

Author Unknown[1]

Foreword

The prayers in this book will tell you much about my late husband, Kenneth Kuntz. He, like the rest of us, dealt with failure, success, joy, sorrow.

I heard often, so remember well, words Ken used almost as a motto: "Keep the faith; tell the story." His conviction was that those two phrases describe activities that cannot be separated. *The Witness* is a product of Ken's steadfastness in both nurturing faith and sharing it.

Support for Ken's growth in faith came from many sources. The Methodist congregation in which he was baptized at the age of nine or ten aroused his childhood ambition to be a church school teacher or an elder. By reading to him early and providing good books, Kenneth's mother helped to develop his appreciation for literature and the arts. A professor of religion in a church-related college challenged him to think deeply and to decide to become a minister in the Christian Church (Disciples of Christ). Oberlin Seminary provided an interdenominational, interracial experience; and the Congregational Church at Amherst, Ohio, which Kenneth served as student pastor, further enriched his formation. Again and again, the Scriptures raised up guideposts to help him rediscover and maintain his way.

Ken's faith led him to test and frequently judge society and the church. He felt it necessary to be involved, seeking to redress the needs of the poor, the hungry, the poorly clad, the unemployed, the illiterate, and the affluent. He believed that unity was a requirement of God's creation.

I was touched when Roy L. Griggs, pastor of First Christian Church in Tulsa, Oklahoma, who knew Ken well, preached a sermon entitled "Keep the Faith—Tell the Story," and sent me the manuscript. Roy was reared in Hannibal, Missouri, while Ken was the pastor of the First Christian Church there, and understood both sides of my husband's personality—the outward one of personal strength and the inward one of tenderness (the better part). After capsuling Ken's career as a pastor and as president of the Disciples' Division of Homeland Ministries in Indianapolis, Roy observed:

"Kenneth was not always easy to get along with. He was, at times, a stubborn Prussian. But those of us who knew him over the years were far more impressed with his warm and vulnerable side. He was a pastor at heart, and somehow the bureaucracy could never efface that instinct.

Roy told how Ken frequently would use "keep the faith; tell the story" as a farewell to a friend after a visit to his office, at home, or at a church gathering. "Those were not random words," he said. "They reflected the faith journey of a great Christian over a distinguished forty-year ministry. They were the culmination of the spiritual search, the biblical study, and the intellectual grappling with great precepts of the Christian faith. These words represent the fundamental task and unique opportunity of Christians in any generation."

In the short time between retirement and his death on October 17, 1984, Kenneth had three special joys.

The garden was planted at the cottage where we had vacationed for thirty years. There was time to fish, enjoy the outdoors, visit with friends and neighbors, and observe the blooming of flowers planted a year before.

Third Christian Church in Indianapolis, his own congregation, employed Ken part-time as minister of administration. Working with a congregation and with a pastor he loved gave his retirement added dimension.

He was invited to speak at the dedication of the Barton Warren Stone Conference Room at the Missions Building, which houses general offices of the Christian Church in Indianapolis. Delivered on October 11, 1983, the address was entitled "The Venerable Stone."

Ken entered the hospital the next day and although he made a great effort, he never recovered. We spent the last five months at our cottage in Minnesota. He was not able to be outside, but enjoyed the beauty about him, read much, listened to favorite music. Ken was a quiet man of few words, and that time was no exception. He did say, "This isn't how we planned it, but it is good."

Two weeks before Ken died we chartered a plane to return to Indianapolis. As the ambulance attendants took him from the cottage to go to the airport, Ken looked up and said, "Keep the faith; tell the story."

Those words came back to me often. When I opened his attache´ after his death, there was a letter for me, a part of which said, "Your joyful and pleasant spirit, frank yet loving counsel, deep faith in God, and love for people have enriched our lives." Humbling. Gratifying. I miss Ken terribly, but always with me, prompting my endeavor, is the challenge: "Keep the faith; tell the story."

Ruth Kuntz

Contents

Introduction

There are two purposes for these meditations. The first is to lead the reader to realize the need for and the means of making a worthy contribution to the Christian life through a personal witness for Christ. Our Lord was a witness for all that God had revealed to him. In much the same sense, we, in our daily living, are responsible to witness for Christ. Each of us leaves a record of what we have seen, heard, and experienced. For the Christian there is the constant challenge to develop our record by means of thought, word, and deed.

The second purpose is to provide a climax for two earlier books—*The Pilgrim* and *The Pioneer*. Each of those volumes sets forth an integral part of the Christian life. *The Pilgrim* is based upon the wilderness-temptation experience of our Lord and was designed to lead the reader to identify with the attitude of the Christian pilgrim who does not ask to see either the way or the goal of life. The pilgrim is content with life lived under God's guidance. *The Pioneer* is set against the background of the parables of our Master. These succinct teachings of Jesus give clear evidence that our Savior knew who was leading his life and the goal toward which his life was moving. There is an aggressive and positive mood about the parables. These teachings reflect the spirit of the pioneer who knows under whose orders he moves.

Every Christian is something of a composite of the spirit of the pilgrim and of the pioneer. These two attitudes mingle in differing intensity in each person to the end that the Christian makes manifest a witness for Christ. The force of Christian faith produces evidence of that faith in every life-situation. The Christian attests to faith in times of joy, peace, and success, as well as in the conditions of grief, anxiety, sorrow, loss, and defeat. Under every situation and in every clime, Christians are under obligation to "stand up" for the faith that is in us and for the Lord whom we have confessed.

I

God Calls Us
to
Witness

A Chosen People

Read: Isaiah 43:10-13;
Acts 9:10-19

". . . he is a chosen instrument of mine
to carry my name. . . ."
Acts 9:15b

God has chosen us. Upon this fact we as Christians build our lives, which are more a recognition of God's choosing us than our choosing God. The pilgrim follows the Eternal leading and the Christian pioneer is under divine direction. Since the Christian is a composite of the spirit of the pilgrim and the pioneer, the result of electing to do God's will does not originate with us. Our place is one of action or re-action upon what God has made evident to God's children.

Written into the fabric of the Bible, the history of the church, and the nature of Christ's revelation of God is the supreme fact that God has chosen us. The very word "chosen" has, in its original meaning, a force of the identity of the chooser in the life and person of the chosen. God has chosen us because God's very spirit is in us, and because God has something of himself at stake in our lives.

Isaiah, in describing the "servant of the Lord," declared, "'You are my witnesses,' says the LORD, 'and my servant whom I have chosen, that you may know and believe me and understand that I am He'" (Isaiah 43:10). This is the expression of One who has an interest in our lives. We are not chosen by some remote accident, but by the design of the Eternal. God's choosing is, therefore, a personal relationship and a continuing situation. God is forever bending toward us that we might respond to that power which is outside our lives, yet strangely within each of us.

The evidence that we are a chosen people because we have responded to the call of God through Jesus Christ is abundant. The Bible begins with the assurance that God has selected us for God's purposes. The author of Genesis puts it this way: "Then God said, 'Let us make man in our own image, after our likeness; and let them have dominion over the fish of the sea, and over the birds of the air, and over the cattle, and over all the earth, and over

3

every creeping thing that creeps upon the earth'" (Genesis 1:26). These words would lead us to believe that we are chosen because we are an integral part of God's plan and that, without us, God's work will not be complete.

The church is composed in every age of those who have been chosen of God and who have accepted the nature of their chosenness. The fact that the church has existed under nearly impossible conditions is sufficient to tell us that it is not a human product but arises out of the purposes of God. Further, the church is a means by which God reaches out to touch human lives. " In the perspective of history, the Church stands out as the most remarkable institution or group of institutions the world has ever seen. If, in the most general and inclusive way, we define the Church as the whole company of those who have publicly confessed their allegiance to the God who has revealed Himself in Christ, we can say that it has persisted as a strong and effective focus of men's loyalty longer than any nation which is prominent in the modern world. Some other religious movements, notably in the East, can make a similar claim, but they have not shown a like ability to maintain themselves amid sweeping changes and to take root among people of the most diverse race, language, nation, and level of culture."[2] The church stands the test of the ages as the instrument through which God chooses us. And we are chosen by the presence of the Divine to work with him through the church.

The revelation of God through Jesus Christ stands as eloquent testimony that we are chosen of God. We need remember no more than that which we learned as children in the church school to know that Jesus is the instrument through which God moves toward us. We all recall the words we were taught from the Gospel of John: "For God so loved the world that he gave his only Son, that whoever believes in him should not perish but have eternal life" (John 3:16). God gave to us before we were able to give to him. The fact is that God revealed himself to us before we were asked to believe in him. The majestic life of our Savior is the climax of the spirit of the Eternal seeking to claim its own. Jesus is the finger of God reaching out to touch our weary, confused lives and to choose us to be with God.

Perhaps no one has ever felt this act of God's choosing more pointedly than did Paul. The grand design behind the Damascus

4

Road experience is set forth in the conversation between the Lord and the disciple Ananias in these words: "he (Paul) is a chosen instrument of mine to carry my name." We may say that this was an isolated experience that means nothing to us today. Lest we brush aside the words of our Lord to Ananias, we need to remember the words of George Santayana who declared, "God must be...truth personified."[3] Truth once established takes on eternal quality. The assertion that Paul was a "chosen instrument" of God to carry the name of Jesus is a truth that falls upon each of us not because we choose God but because God first chose us. Because God has chosen us we are called to bear God's name and bear witness through our lives. As pilgrim and as pioneer, let us accept our chosenness and give ourselves to the establishment of a viable witness of all that we have seen and heard and known through all we think, speak, and do.

PRAYER:

O Lord, thou hast witnessed for us in the acts of creation, in the gift of thy church, and in the revealing of thyself through thy Son, Jesus Christ. Deliver us from the presumptiveness that we can choose thee before thou choosest us. Stir within our souls the awareness that thy image is in us and that thou dost choose us because thy spirit yearns to be united with such of thy presence as is within us. Magnify thy power in our lives that it may consume us. Then, O God, let the beauty of thy ways be the testimony of our lives because we have been chosen of thee and, in humble gratitude, we have chosen thee. In the name of our Lord, Jesus Christ, whose life is testimony of thy choosing us, we pray. Amen.

God's Witness

Read: Job 16:18-22

> *"And he who sent me is with me;*
> *he has not left me alone . . . . "*
>
> John 8:29a

God is our witness. This means God will testify in our behalf. The full force of this fact is set forth by Job who had listened to the diatribe of his pious friends. Miserable as he was, Job knew the purity in his own heart. Despised and rejected by men he cried out, "Even now, behold, my witness is in heaven, and he that vouches for me is on high" (Job 16:19). The Eternal witnesses for us, and though we do not always comprehend the words, the fullness of time will reveal his testimony.

God's witness is an effective power in the midst of our human relationships. When Jacob and his father-in-law Laban were having disagreements, they called upon God to be a witness between them. These men did not trust each other, but they both trusted the oversight of God. Agreeing upon the witness of God, Jacob and Laban declared,

> The LORD watch between you and me, when we
> are absent one from the other.
>
> Genesis 31:49b

God stands as a witness unto his righteousness in the life of the individual and in human affairs.

God's witness was the sustaining power of our Lord. Jesus was pressed to identify himself as a part of the Messianic tradition. Part of his evidence was stated in these words: "When you have lifted up the Son of man, then you will know that I am he, and that I do nothing on my own authority but speak thus as the Father taught me. And he who sent me is with me; he has not left me alone" (John 8:28-29a). The assurance that God had not forsaken his Son gave Jesus the power to accept the pilgrimage that was unfolding before him and, in like manner, was the sustaining power through our Master's ministry.

God witnesses to us in our own time. As Jesus was drawing near the end of his earthly experience he sensed the despair of the disciples. In the upper room sermon, our Lord spoke to the need of his followers in this manner: "If you love me, you will keep my commandments. And I will pray the Father, and he will give you another Counselor, to be with you for ever, even the Spirit of truth, whom the world cannot receive, because it neither sees him nor knows him; you know him, for he dwells with you, and will be in you" (John 14:15-17). The Christian is assured that God will continue to witness for every time in our lives.

In these few instances we learn that God does not leave us alone. God continues, through the "Spirit of truth," to witness for us. As a result we confidently accept God's choosing of us and, in turn, choose God. It is not enough that we have been chosen by the Eternal. In our recognition of such a choosing, we, in turn, must complete the circle of life and choose God. It is in our act of choosing God that we see most clearly God's witness to us.

Moses was a faltering tool, wavering in decision and trembling before the choosing of God, until it was made clear to him that God would be constant in his witnessing. Noah knew that he had been chosen to do the will of Jehovah. However, it was not until Noah saw the rainbow-tinted sky that he realized the extent of God's continuous witness. When Jesus hung upon the cross he cried out, "My God, my God, why hast thou forsaken me?" (Matthew 27:46b). But before the darkness of death overcame the Christ, the witness of the Father had penetrated his tortured body and our Lord cried out, "Father into thy hands I commit my spirit!" (Luke 23:46b).

The choosing of God is followed with his everlasting witness to us. It remains for us to be able to accept both the choosing and the witness of our heavenly Father. Then shall we understand the words of the psalmist when he said,

> If I ascend to heaven, thou art there!
> If I make my bed in Sheol, thou art there!
> Psalm 139:8

God's choosing of us is no less everlasting than his witnessing to us. Both are constant, ever-present, and without ceasing. As pilgrims and pioneers of the Christian way, we are recipients of the witness of the love, life, and purpose of the Divine. We are challenged to accept the selection of our God and witness for God as God has witnessed for us.

Thou, O God, whose "love wilt not let us go," we beseech thee that thy everlasting witness may penetrate our hearts. Stab our minds into wakefulness, that our thoughts may be full of thee. Possess our souls that we may behold no image but thy presence and give ourselves to no task save that of thy kingdom. We implore thee, our Father, that we may never close our minds to thy thoughts or turn our hands from thy labors. For, as thou hast been faithful in thy witness to us, so, O Lord, let us be dedicated unto thee in our choosing first thy "kingdom and its righteousness." This we pray in the name of our Master who found no nobler task than to bear witness to thee. Amen.

Chosen to Persevere

Read: Hebrews 12:1-2

> *". . . run with perseverance the race that
> is set before us . . . . "*
> Hebrews 12:1d

We are chosen to persevere in our Christian witness. The ability to press on springs from adequate preparation, a determined earnestness, and the action described in "keeping on keeping on." The poet has described the nature of perseverance as follows:

> Less good from genius we may find
>   Than that from perseverance flowing;
> So have good grist at hand to grind,
>   And keep the mill a-going.[4]

The task of being a witness for Christ is of such a nature that, for many of us, only human perseverance, upheld by the constant witness of God, will see us through to victory. To keep on when others fail and our own soul falters is the human contribution to the expression of our faith. When Paul wrote to the proud people of Corinth, he said,

> Five times I have received...the forty lashes less one. Three times I have been beaten with rods; once I was stoned. Three times I have been shipwrecked...in danger from rivers,...danger from robbers, danger from my own people, ...danger in the city, danger in the wilderness...in toil and hardship.... And, apart from other things, there is the daily pressure upon me of my anxiety for all the churches.
>
> 2 Corinthians 11:24-29

The master missionary was leading the people of Corinth to understand that there is no substitute for standing firm in the face of all difficulties. No amount of culture, tradition, or pride can lift us over the obstacles of living as can the willingness to

> ...have good grist at hand ...,
> And keep the mill a-going.

Beyond our sense of determination, perseverance is maintained by an awareness that our witnessing is based upon earnest commitment. The kind of commitment needed by the Christian witness was evident in one of the regiments of the 9th Infantry Division in 1943. Just before the regiment was to assault Sicily, there appeared on every helmet and truck in the entire regiment the letters "AAA-O." When General Omar N. Bradley asked, "And just what does that mean?" he was told, "Anything, anytime, anywhere, bar nothing—that's what it means." The development of the life of the pilgrim and the pioneer is more than grinding determination. It is the high resolve of earnest commitment. Emil Brunner described a noble concept for all who would press on in Christian witness when he said, "One needs courage, love of adventure, to sail into the unknown dangers of the open sea. Here is the field for the pioneer who is not afraid to stand alone, to swim against the stream and to take a course hateful to the mass of those who are bound by tradition."[5]

When, as Christians, we accept the choosing of God and become witnesses for him, we will be living as we sing,

9

It may not be on the mountain height,
Or over the stormy sea,
It may not be at the battle's front
My Lord will have need of me;
But if, by a still, small voice
He calls to paths that I do not know,
I'll answer, dear Lord, with my hand in Thine,
I'll go where you want me to go.[6]

PRAYER:

Dear God, thou hast called us to live and speak for thee. In all that thou hast given us to do, we beseech thee to keep open the fountains of thy power that though we are weak we shall be strong, though we falter thou wilt gather us up, though we fail thou wilt show us new tasks to do. We do not ask to escape the peril of our tasks. We do pray that we shall have the human determination and the spiritual undergirding of thy presence to the end that our witness shall be acceptable upon this earth and in heaven. Amen.

We Are Called at Personal Risk

Read: Revelation 20:4-6

*"Also I saw the souls of those who had been
beheaded for their testimony to Jesus and
for the word of God . . . . "*
Revelation 20:4b

The Greek word for witness by a profound instinct was appropriated to those who had borne witness by the wounds that had won them martyrdom. Their tombs bore, not the signs of cruel death, but triumphant resurrection. We, like the first century Christians, are called to witness for Christ at great personal risk. John, the author of the book of Revelation, spoke out of the crucible of human suffering as a prisoner of Rome on the island of Patmos. This man was bearing in his body the "wounds" of his witness. By this example, he was able to demonstrate that we are called to witness for Christ at great personal risk.

When Dr. and Mrs. A.L. Shelton sailed from San Francisco in September of 1903, there was no hint of the cost they were to pay for the response they were making to witness for Christ as missionaries in Tibet. As the years moved on, the work began to grow in Tatsienlu. The tragic result was that Dr. Shelton lost his life in the act of carrying out his testimony. He had paid a high price to witness for Christ.

While many, as John said in his vision, are "beheaded for their testimony to Jesus," there are vast numbers of others who discover there is great personal risk in testifying for Christ, and that in ways other than facing death. One such person was Roger, a young man of fine ability and high scholarship. It had been his desire from childhood to become a lawyer. Roger worked to secure enough money to enter college. Early in his first year at college, Roger returned home saying, "I cannot go on in my study of law. I must study to be a minister." When we determine to witness for Christ, we find our life's directions changed. Though such changes are costly in time and money, we recognize we are called to witness at great personal risk.

Despite the risks involved, there is no real peace for our lives until we respond affirmatively to God's calling. The Lord calls us in many and diverse ways. It remains for us to be alert to this calling. Robert Frost, the poet, points up the necessity to submit willingly to God's leading:

> Something we were withholding made us weak
> Until we found out that it was ourselves
> We were withholding from our land of living,
> And forthwith found salvation in surrender.[7]

It is at this point of surrender that what seems great personal risk to others becomes the opening portal to our inner peace. Perhaps no man suffered greater hardships as a pilgrim-pioneer of our Lord than did David Livingstone. Yet, no one found greater inner peace than did he who brought to Africa its first bright hope. Livingstone had responded to the calling of God. Chosen to witness for Christ, and linked with human surrender, the proper tribute to his life was made when the vast congregation at his memorial services sang,

> Oh God of Bethel, by whose hand
> Thy people still are fed;
> Who through this weary pilgrimage
> Hast all our fathers led.[8]

Whatever the risk, it is small compared to the inner peace and outward glory of lifting an acceptable testimony "to Jesus and for the word of God."

PRAYER:

Thou, O God, hast called us to a noble task of witnessing for thee. We are glad we accepted thy choosing before knowing all our task would cost us. Now, as we begin to sense how great the risk will be, O Lord, deliver us from craven fear. Let not our hearts grow numb or our hands grow cold. In the darkness of our greatest doubt let us feel "thy everlasting arms" beneath us and sense thy brooding love 'round us. Let the light of thy holy presence shine before us and lead us that we may never lose hope. In all, our Father, may we have a sense of inner peace because we have willingly accepted thy choosing. At last, let us see the risk is never greater than the victory or the inner distress stronger than thy strengthening peace. Amen.

We Are Called to a Full Witness

Read: John 3:1-15

> *"Truly, truly, I say to you, we speak of what*
> *we know, and bear witness to what*
> *we have seen . . . ."*
> John 3:11a

God chooses us to witness for him. Though imperfect in knowledge and incomplete in experience, we are asked to use our every ability to stand for our Lord. The possibility of our development and the spirit with which we testify makes us worthy of God's drawing us out to serve him. Jesus, speaking to Nicodemus, reflects concern for what this young man did not know and for the lack of the pilgrim-pioneer spirit that he evidenced.

We have been selected to know God. This firsthand understanding of the heavenly Father is imperative. Peter, the big fisherman, had been with Jesus. As the faithful apostle sought to lead the early church, this intimate knowledge was an invaluable asset that Peter described this way:

> For we did not follow cleverly devised myths when we made known to you the power and coming of our Lord Jesus Christ, but we were eyewitnesses of his majesty.
>
> 2 Peter 1:16

The tragedy of Nicodemus was that he knew the writings and records of the law, but he did not know the spirit of the Christ. Such a lack of understanding made this young man an unfit witness. To the contrary, Jesus points out the close relationship needed for a full witness of his power as we read,

> Take my yoke upon you, and learn from me....
>
> Matthew 11:29a

If we are to bear a testimony worthy of even human notice, it must spring from our being "harnessed" with our Lord and learning from him.

Though we possess, as Paul said, "all knowledge...but have not love, (we are) nothing" (1 Corinthians 13). For every witness-fire there must be a spark of spirit that lights the tinder of the soul. The spark of love for God must set aflame our whole being to the end that we witness in all we see, hear, and experience through all we think, speak, and do. We are called to be complete witnesses of the fullness of God's truth revealed through Jesus Christ.

The impact of such inclusive witness is seen in human affairs today when we read what Whitaker Chambers wrote in his controversial volume, *Witness*:

The revolutionary heart of Communism is not the
theatrical appeal: "Workers of the world, unite.
You have nothing to lose but your chains. You
have a world to gain." It is a simple statement of
Karl Marx, further simplified for hand use: "Phi-
losophers have explained the world; it is necessary to change the world."[9]

This is no limpid appeal to half-hearted, semi-dedicated people
to do what they can. This is the explosive power of revolution let
loose to set persons in a new orbit of human behavior. The
statement in itself is not so amazing as the contemplation of the
vast reaches of spiritual drive that are called to exert themselves
upon human life as a result of the challenge. This is the immense
passion that can consume persons and use them for human advantage.

The pilgrim-pioneer Christian is drawn out to answer a
similar high commitment of deep spiritual motivation. It was
none other than our Lord who said,

Follow me and I will make you become fishers of
men.

Mark 1:17

Go therefore and make disciples of all nations,
baptizing (and) ...teaching....

Matthew 28:19-20

Our Master set before us the task of "changing the world." To
this work we must bring to bear the best of our knowledge and
understanding linked with fervent spirits that will give light to our
confused lives. It is the labor of all witnesses to give the fullness
of ourselves to the wholeness of our testimony. Only in such
attitude can we hope to find meaning for our personal living and,
at the same time, "change the world" for the good of humankind
and the glory of God.

PRAYER:

We give thee thanks, O God, that thou art one. In thy single
self we see the hope of all we want to be. Forgive us when we
reject thine own image which is in us and strive to divide our
knowledge and spirit to do many things rather than one thing.

Deliver us from the paltry satisfaction of achievements in many areas. Earnestly do we beseech thee to place in our lives both the understanding of thy truth and the burning spirit to witness to that truth. Capture our minds and hearts and souls to the end our witness of thee may be a pure flaming light which is unshielded by our human desires and unquenchable by our divisive natures. In thought and word and deed may we pray and work that "the words of our lips and the meditations of our minds" and the deeds of our hands may be acceptable in thy sight, O Lord, our strength and our redeemer. Amen.

To this point we have been led to recognize we are chosen persons. God has designated us to bear his mark upon our lives through Christian witness of our faith, knowledge, and understanding of God through our every thought, word, and deed. Any such recognition is only the beginning of all that must come through the years of living.

As those chosen of God, let us search out the times and ways of our witnessing. Far too frequently, we are given to despair because we believe only certain gifted people can testify for God. The fact is each of us has evidence to give, and we are called upon daily to make known that which is our faith. We are chosen to speak and live in the normal, everyday experiences that life brings to us. In our emotions, in our homes, in our victories and defeats, in our joy and sorrow, in our health and illness, in our labor and leisure, in every area and place of human experience and endeavor, God expects us to witness for him. Let us address ourselves to a closer searching out of the witness that is ours in the fullness of life.

II

In Love
and When Love
Disappoints

God's Gift of Love

Read: 1 John 4:7-12

". . .if we love one another, God abides in us
and his love is perfected in us."
1 John 4:12b

God's love is a matchless gift that abides in us. We are not the object of God's love because we deserve it, or are good enough to receive it, or wise enough to understand it. We are loved of God because it is God's nature to love us and he can do no less. The writer of 1 John is perfectly correct in observing "for God is love" (1 John 4:8b). God has underlaid our feet with treasures abundant in the earth. God has o'er shaded us with the blessings of the sun and moon and stars. Our God has surrounded us with the necessities of human existence beyond our fondest hopes and quite beyond our imagination to share properly. Finally, God has implanted himself in our very beings. When we rejected all that was done for us, Perfect Love would not be denied. God revealed himself to us through Jesus Christ. Our Master did bear our sins and remain spotless; he died for us and overcame death. All this and much more is the gift of God in each of us chosen to witness of him.

Our God chooses us to be with him upon this earth and eternally. To be with God is no small thing. It means we are caught up in all the power, strength, and love of the Divine. We are called to walk and talk with God in the knowledge that never again will we stand in the devastating loneliness of our own strength. Though enemies may encircle us and though friends may fail us, we have, at least, found the company of One who will never leave us alone. The most magnificent evidence of our togetherness with our Lord is the fact that we are recipients of this love.

Awareness of the fact that love is God's gift to us stands as a special part of human experience. Too long we have been induced to believe that love is some shallow emotion, some force derived of the power of human thought, or the extension of some unconscious functioning of the psyche. In the trammels of these misconceptions we have not alone rejected the true nature of love, but we have broken the ties with the Eternal that God has sought to establish. We have thought we could make love work for us when it must become evident that we must let love work through us as it will.

Man must become the captive of love. George Matheson understood this fact clearly. At the age of eighteen he was totally blind. During the evening of June 6, 1882, as he sat alone in his study at Innellan, he was suddenly inspired to compose a poem. George Matheson had become engaged to a young woman who broke the engagement because of the blindness and married another man. Out of this tragedy came the hymn that is sung throughout the world.[10] George Matheson discovered he was the captive of love that was God's gift to him, and he wrote...

> O Love that wilt not let me go,
> I rest my weary soul in thee;
> I give thee back the life I owe,
> That in thine ocean depth its flow
> May richer, fuller be.

God chooses us and then gives us the gift of his eternal love. He gives it to us when we do not know how to reach out for it. And John is correct in saying, "In this is love, not that we loved God but that he loved us and sent his Son to be the expiation for our sins (1 John 4:10).

PRAYER:

How, O Lord, couldst thou choose us, we who are without goodness or wisdom or hope! We are amazed that though we are desolate, bewildered, and confused, thou hast let the mantle of thy presence fall upon us. We do not fathom the depths of thy love; but we eagerly reach out the empty hands of our souls to accept this matchless gift. Lord, when by the power of thy love for us, we learn how to walk upright and speak boldly for thee, then O God, deliver us from any sense of pride that would lead us to believe we are good or true or pure or holy. In the surrounding and upholding power of thy loving presence, let us be content to live. Lord, let us accept thy gift of love and be content that, as it passes through us and moves about us, our lives may "richer, fuller be." Amen.

The Eternal Nature of Love

Read: 1 Corinthians 13:1-8a

"Love never ends . . . ."
1 Corinthians 13:8a

"My love for my wife has died." This is the statement heard by not a few of those who seek to keep the covenant of marriage sacred. No utterance is so filled with lack of understanding of the nature of love than the words, "Love has died." Robert Southey puts the matter in metered form:

> They sin who tell us love can die;
> With life all other passions fly,
> All others are but vanity.
> Love is indestructible,
> Its holy flame forever burneth;
> From heaven it came, to heaven returneth ....[11]

Paul catches up the same theme when he describes the pertinent qualities of love and rises to the brilliant climax in his letter to the Christians at Corinth by asserting, "Love never ends."

The eternal nature of love stems from the fact that it is the very nature of God, and since God is eternal, his nature of love is indestructible. An ancient sage portrayed the nature of love with these words, "Love is like the hull of a ship. Though covered with barnacles and the life of the sea, when cleared the hull remains the same." Amid all change, love is changeless.

The transitory nature of our human existence calls for a firm foundation. God's gift of eternal love, amid all our passing passions and fancies, is the one rock for any real hope or stable life. When we exchange the vows that form the covenant of marriage, we make a mockery of our language and betray the home, the church, and the conscience of the community unless we predicate our contract upon the eternal nature of love. Love is the only power that can stabilize life when the impatience and unkindness of those nearest to us seek to quilt the mind in meanness. Love is the only hope for the unity of life when the levers of pride and jealousy would tear us apart. Love is that majestic quality that leads us to believe the best when we know the worst, to hope for the fullest when we have the least, to bear the heaviest burdens when we have the faintest strength, and to endure the "fiery darts of the evil one" when we have no faith equal to his power. Love, God's gift, courses through our souls reviving and stabilizing us just as fresh air revives one dying with smoke-clogged lungs. This eternal love of God pulses through us and binds us together, providing our trembling lives with hope and faith and spiritual strength. It is upon this undying, indestructible love that our lives must rest or we sink into the pit of despair and the mire of oblivion.

Wherever this quality of love has touched the world and human life, its concentric circles never cease to move. Henry Drummond in *The Greatest Thing in the World* has put it this way: "In the heart of Africa, among the great Lakes, I have come across black men and women who remembered the only white man they ever saw before—David Livingstone; and as you cross his footsteps in that dark continent, men's faces light up as they speak of the kind Doctor who passed there years ago. They could not understand him, but they felt the Love that beat in his heart.[12] This is the love that refuses to die. And for those who think it has died must come the terrible knowledge they have somehow lost God and his love or else never been possessed of him.

Those who would witness of God must accept his gift of love and be constantly immersed in the eternal nature of that love. This is the universal language that all broken hearts and sundered relationships gasp to possess. Lift your witness to the love that is in you and not of you, the love that will not die.

PRAYER:

O God, whose nature is love eternal, breathe into our barren lives of hopelessness the spirit of thy presence which knows not the bonds of death. Free us from the feeble thought that love belongs to us or that it is the creature of our making. Teach us that love is not the child of our wanting or the product of our passion. Lord, may we understand that love is not so much perceived by the mind or acknowledged by the senses as it is the movement of thy spirit which would embrace us and hold us fast to thee. As we are drawn to thee by the bonds of thy eternal love, Lord, may we be united with and become a uniting part of thy kingdom upon this earth. In this love, may we dwell in peace with thee and in the power of hope with those who are nearest to us and with those who are far from us. This we pray in the name of our Lord, Jesus Christ, who knew and manifested the eternalness of love. Amen.

The Transforming Power of Love

Read: Luke 7:36-50

". . .for she loved much . . . ."
Luke 7:47a

Love produces change and change is frequently painful. Birth is change both for the child and for the mother, and pain is a part of birth. Death is the culmination of the process of transforming the body from life to lifelessness, and pain is involved. Love is a transforming power in human life. When two people fall in love with each other there is much joy, but the new relationships of happiness leave in their wake the fretted waters of human hurt. As the new family is formed, there develops an altered condition with the parents and childhood homes. Old friends may no longer fit into the new situations. These changes are frequently painful to the individual. This does not mean the new relationships will be less. As a matter of fact, the new conditions may well become a higher fulfillment and a nobler development of love.

As love transforms the individual in the personal relationships of marriage, as much must be observed in the deeper qualities of love that transform our ideals and habits. No person in all the New Testament shows the evidence of the transforming power of love so effectively as does the life of Mary of Magdala. Love, for Mary Magdalene, as for everyone, meant giving herself away. It is as Carlyle said in reference to Tyndale, "give yourself royally." This in itself is a radical change because more often than not, we seek to protect and keep ourselves. Mary knew the hollowness of self-love that gives but never receives, satisfies itself only to be forever dissatisfied, used by others but exalted by none. She wanted to give herself away but did not know to whom or how. Only in giving her life to Jesus did she discover the transforming power of love.

In the process of transformation, Mary of Magdala gave herself to Jesus the man. Others had sought to use this woman. Now she had found one who respected her as a person. In gratitude for this highest of all gifts—self-respect—Mary gave Jesus the finest of her possessions. Her witness of change was evident as she "brought an alabaster flask of ointment...and anointed" Jesus. With her tears she testified to the altered life that was taking form. Undoubtedly these were tears of repentance and of joy, mingled and flowing down to tell all of both her shame and her enfolding of new life.

But love is never content to bind us to persons. Mary Magdalene discovered this, too, because she gave herself to Jesus the Christ. Through the love that Jesus expressed in her as a person, Mary first sensed the eternal depth of that which binds us with God. The fact that she held nothing back, but gave her proudest possession—even to her tears and humility—is eloquent evidence that here was love that had wrought its work completely.

Love has the greatest pulling power in the world. It forever tugs at us to make us not so much discontent with what we are as to make us the fulfillment of all we want to be. For, when we love, we want to be the best those who love us believe we are. To love Jesus is not simply to give ourselves to him, but to strive to be what he wants us to be. Herein is the transforming power of love. Though the change may cost us dearly and though the seeking may lead us in difficult ways, it still remains as the greatest of all commendations that anyone may say of us "...for (he) loved much...."

PRAYER:

Dear God, we plead for the spirit of thy love which alone can transform us from what we are into that which, by thy grace, we can and ought to be. Deliver us from selfish thoughts and deeds wherein we believe we have satisfied our desires only to discover we have become imprisoned in the hateful and possessive will of others. Pour out upon our lives that spirit of love, whereby we give ourselves to thee, through thy Son, Jesus Christ. Let our lives become an emerging and enlarging testimony of our devotion to Jesus the man and to Jesus the Christ. Consume us in thy love, O God, that evil may be smothered in our lives, and pure light of thy truth become the evidence of our years. Amen.

When Love Disappoints

Read: Matthew 16:5-12

> *"O men of little faith, why do you discuss*
> *among yourselves the fact that you*
> *have no bread?"*
> Matthew 16:8b

Love, being outgoing by nature, is ever in danger of disappointment. Never protecting itself, love is vulnerable to misunderstanding, misinterpretation, and misappropriation. Our Lord was frequently brought to the state of lamentation because those nearest to him did not understand the objective nature nor the purpose of his love. Jesus gave them the "bread of life" and they sought to fill their physical hunger. The Son of God showed them the kingdom of God and they dreamed of that kingdom wherein one would sit on the right and the other on the left as Jesus ruled. He endeavored to give his followers an understanding of the Messiah as the extension of God's will working in them, and the disciples saw him as the force to overthrow the Roman oppressors.

The love of God expressed through Jesus or human love expressed to others always leaves the lover defenseless. The nature of love is such that the lover never defends himself, but endeavors to expend himself in expressing love. In World War II four chaplains willingly gave their life jackets to others and went down with their ship. Alexander D. Good, the Jew; Father John P. Washington, the Roman Catholic; George L. Fox and Clark Poling, the Protestants, will be remembered for their witness to Christian love. The act of these selfless men has been called "heroic" and "epic." It is all of this and more. This is one of those crystal-clear witnesses of love that leaves in its wake the wash of anguish and the upward current of newfound faith. This is love that cannot defend itself and must suffer.

Love always has open arms and an open heart. We can see evidences of this in everyday life. Mrs. Smathers was a woman with open arms and an open heart. Her marriage left much to be desired because her husband was less than responsible and frequently dissipated their meager income in strong drink. Mrs. Smathers never sought to break the marriage covenant. In speaking of the matter a few months after her husband's death she said, "Of course, I could have secured a divorce, but when we were married I took a vow in which I said, 'for better, for worse.' My husband turned out worse instead of better. Yet I loved him and I would never set him aside." This woman's love had caused her shame in the community, intense personal disappointment, and had reduced her life to making the family income by working as a domestic in the homes of the community. For her, love had disappointed, but her witness of love shone all the brighter because she kept her vows.

Love does not consider anything but the object of its love. It remains for the little person to think only of self and of "bread." To those who discover the wonder of love remains the joy of rising above all human hurt and shame. Love seems to move through and beyond all disappointment until it enjoins itself with the very nature of God. Here the restless find rest, and the misunderstanding, misinterpretation, and misappropriation of life fades away. Through the sorrow of love's hurt is to be found the only real value of life. Robert Browning has put it clearly for us in these words:

> What if the rose-streak of morning
> Pale and depart in a passion of tears?
> Once to have hoped is no matter for scorning!
> Love once—e'en love's disappointment endears!
> A minute's success pays the failure of the years.[13]

26

Thou lover of our souls, teach us how to love as thou hast loved us. Deliver us, O Lord, from the love of bread, drink, dwelling, and things. Let our hearts be open to the pulsing of thy love. In the rhythm of thy love, let our arms and hearts be open to thee and to others. By thy mercy lead us, O God, to dare to suffer as thou didst suffer with thy Son on Calvary that love may work its wonder in our hearts. Let us shun not the hurt and disappointment lest we lose the glory of thy face and the power of thy presence. Even in the crushing moments of our grief which love has brought, let us sense the power of thy cradling arms that would teach us to love and show us how to live for and with thee. Amen.

Love's Victory

Read: John 13:31-35

" . . .*love one another*. . . ."
John 13:34a

Love is eternal. Unhampered by the limitations of time and space, love coexists with God. The victory of love is assured in the nature of the divine. When Jesus was taking his leave of the disciples before the betrayal and crucifixion, a new commandment was given, "...love one another." Here was more than a rule by which to live. It was a celestial description of victory over life and assurance of eternal life. This grand affirmation of what life can be at its best leaves unspoken the darker realms of life where love does not exist.

Each of us can sense the "length, breadth, height, and depth" of God's love for us, which is expressed through Jesus Christ. Yet, we must do more than sense this love. There is high need for us to embody this love in our daily lives. Thereby we become prisoners of the way of God and are incorporated into God's presence. The "how" of this kind of love is given meaningfulness when we understand its victory is to be discovered in ourselves, upon this earth, and that it leads us to eternal life.

It is said that Francis of Assissi was an "apostle of love." So gentle was he that the homeless came to him with confidence and even the birds and beasts of the field responded to him as he spoke to them as "brothers." But this was not the way Francis' life began. As the son of a prosperous merchant, he found pleasure in parties and was repulsed by the sight of those who suffered from disease, particularly those whose bodies were mutilated by leprosy. Not until the young Francis embraced a leper was his life changed. He discovered a deep spirit of love in his heart that, when once opened, was a never-ending spring of devotion to those who suffered from leprosy. Love won its victory in this young man's life and transformed all his years into a brilliant anthem of Christian devotion. Such is the discovery that awaits all who,

> Breathless, in the day, they greet
> And fling each other wholly heart to heart.[14]

What love works as a victory inside the individual ultimately finds expression in daily life. The parents of Robert S. Johnstone, Jr. witnessed to the victory of love upon this earth when their son was killed in May 1944, fighting the Japanese. In his memory, his parents established a scholarship at Lafayette College. Japanese applicants were to receive priority. "Our son felt that way about the Japanese," his father explained, adding, "We need to understand the Christian spirit of goodwill." The scholarship was financed by Robert Junior's $10,000 government insurance. The post-war relations between the United States and the Japanese people have proved the validity of this act taken while passions were still hot.[15] When love has its way in our lives, it works its miracle for the good of the individual and for society. And through the veil of disappointment, love sends its shining rays of hope and better life

Love has never finished its work until it binds us inexorably with the person of God. This is the weaving of our lives into the great life of the Eternal, which is not less than eternal life. In love there is no half-victory. It must suffer until victory is complete. Love discloses this matchless glory to us as it did to Alfred

Tennyson a few hours before his death, when rousing from unconsciousness he said:

Out of the darkness of night
The world rolls into light
It is daybreak everywhere.

Love graces the dawn of every life and sets the power of victory moving in each human heart. Though the way is difficult and never without hurt, the result is nothing less than victory for self, for life, and for eternal life.

PRAYER:

Just now, O Lord, I feel that life is too much with me and too heavy to bear. I have sought to love and been rejected, I have tried to continue to love and found only the bitter cup of soul agony, I stretched out my hands in love and they returned empty. Lord, my soul cries out for thy spirit. Deliver me from the darkness of my human despair. Fill me with thy love which thy Son expressed as he wore the crown of thorns and as his body was riven with the spear. Give me such love as will bear me up and will draw those about me into thy fellowship wherein we may truly be one with thee. For thy gift of such love I lift my heart to praise thee and to offer my life to be thy temple, through Jesus Christ my Lord. Amen.

III

In Success and When the Glory Departs

Trademark of Success

Read: Revelation 22:1-5

> *" . . . and his name shall be on their
> foreheads."*
> Revelation 22:4b

John had a vision of human regalness crowned with the glory of God: "and his name shall be on their foreheads." Compare this with the synthetic success for which we expend our daily strength. The ego yearns with a fiery passion to achieve the places of "glory, laud, and honor." Not unlike Daniel Webster, we seek to be first, not knowing that to be less than first may best bring forth the issue of highest order. With the unmastered emotions of an alcoholic, we crave prestige, never understanding that "many that are first will be last, and the last first" (Matthew 19:30). The human crown of success was upon Adolph Hitler as he swept across Europe in the early flush of victory. Alas! We, like him who sought and attained dominion over human beings, must end our time in the small confines of the bunkers of our own unmastered greed.

The American credo of success has perverted the meaning of the word itself. That which is properly a process for the fullest human development has been immersed into a sea of static condition where someone becomes something never to become anything. Surrounding the cult of success is the position of power, the dominance of authority, the possession of things. In sharp contrast to the mass of small meanings that we have called success must stand the over-arching power of God in whom is true glory.

In the Old Testament, the glory of God was indescribable. God's light was so powerful that none dared look upon it and the shrine of the eternal—the Ark—was destructive to the human touch. It was this glory of God that human beings needed and that, when it resided with them, gave success. In the New Testament, the word *doxa* is the word for glory. It means "opinion" or "fame." Jesus sought the opinion and fame of God. So successful was he in this search that he declared, "I and the Father are one" (John 10:30). Again, our Lord identified the matter with the words, "For the Son of man is to come...in the glory of his Father" (Matthew 16:27a).

The word *success* does not appear in the New Testament. Yet the New Testament is one of the noblest success stories ever written. Inscribed by the "fame" of God through the life of Jesus Christ, the "good news" is the record of the man of Nazareth accepting "his name...on (his) forehead." God is the author of success and any other authorship is a forgery. As this high drama rises to its climax at Golgotha there is only darkness, tears, death, and, as James Russell Lowell has said, life might be "Texts of despair or hope, of joy or moan." Out of the "moan" of the crucifixion came the glory of God in the majesty of the resurrection. "And his name shall be on their foreheads."

Tucked away in the writings of the gospels of Mark and Luke are four verses telling of a woman who "out of her poverty put in all the living that she had" into the treasury (Luke 21:4b). The name of the woman is forgotten, but the praise she won from Jesus was glory such as all desire and few secure.

The trademark of human success can be catalogued with membership in exclusive clubs, the distinction of the "grey flannel suit," the home in suburbia, the car of super-horsepower. Compare the fading glory of these few strands of tinsel to the glories that Paul presents in proud array as "the fruit of the Spirit is love, joy, peace, patience, kindness, goodness, faithfulness, gentleness, self-control..." (Galatians 5:22-23a).

Let us seek the trademark of success. Let it be not less than the glory of God "descending upon us" that "his name shall be on (our) foreheads."

PRAYER:

Lord, forgive us for our haughty ways and for our pride in human gain. Purge our souls in the fires of humility that we may become the pure instruments of thy holy will. When we speak, let us be full of shame until we have prostrated our minds before thee that we may utter thy words and not the words of mundane lips. When we act, let us be filled with holy discontent until we seek to let thy "finger" move through our hands to perform thy deeds. When we leap or shout or sing, let it all be to thy "glory, laud, and honor." Lord, we beseech thee, let thy glory be our one desiring, our only claim to success. Amen.

Danger

Read: Judges 11:29-34

*"If thou wilt give the Ammonites into my
hand . . . ."*
Judges 11:30b

What fatal words! "If thou wilt give... into my hand." These words could form the epitaph of much of human history: human grasping, greedy seeking. In this primitive story of ancient religion, Jephthah bargained with God: "...give...into my hand." This has been the point of destruction for many. Just prior to World War II an Englishman said, "All Hitler has taken till now has had some reasonable basis in history. But his march on Poland is reaching for too much!" The beginning of destruction for the Third Reich of Germany was the greedy grasp of "give ...into my hand."

As with nations, so it is with individuals. In the late 1920s, a farmer in northern Iowa had acquired—and paid for—all the land he could profitably use. Seeking still more land, he mortgaged all he had purchased with years of earnest toil. In a few months he had lost all. Across the darkness of human greed comes the throbbing anthem of judgment on all who seek more and more: "Fool! This night your soul is required of you" (Luke 12:20a). Such is the danger of nations and individuals who put their trust in the success visible to human sight. They seek to have treasures delivered into their hands, but are bankrupt in the treasury of heavenly values.

Witness to these fatal words is not confined to nations and individuals. It can be found in the chancel of the church. A recent publication is entitled *Business Handbook for Churches.* One of the great tragedies of the twentieth-century church is that it is managed as a business. It is not unlike the matter of the diplomatic service that is conducted all too frequently by those who can afford the cost rather than by those who love the people of other nations. Pearl Buck, in her autobiographical work, *My Several Worlds,* describes her appraisal of some of the missionaries she knew in China. She has this to say: "And yet I know intuitively that they (the missionaries) were not in China primarily because they loved the people, even though during the years they did learn to love a people naturally loveable."[16] The difference between loving the people and loving a people forms the chasm that Jephthah discovered. The danger of having the Ammonites delivered into his hand with no thought of personal concern was crushed to earth beneath the burden of sorrow when the leader's daughter rushed to greet him. In the church, the same danger lurks—we love humankind, we cannot see the one in need on the doorstep.

The holy life is stifled when we reduce the affairs of God to a business, noting success in terms of profit, numbers, and crowds. God counted loss as nothing when Christ was upon the cross. All the profit was squeezed out of life at Golgotha. The real success of God did not illumine the world until the dawn of resurrection day. At last success was measured as small in relation to the limitless glory of God; yet what victory God had wrought could not be counted in human ledgers.

"Give into my hand" is the cry of those who, like Jack Horner of nursery-rhyme fame, want the world to see "what a good boy am I." We, like Jephthah, lose our greatest treasures when we seek to boast of what we have accomplished. By contrast, our Lord on the cross simply said, "into thy hands I commend my spirit." Danger of destruction awaits those who reject the hand of God to hold in their own hand the staff of victory's banner.

PRAYER:

Forgive us, O Lord, when the best we can do is boast of human deeds or enumerate successes achieved. Steep our lives in the crucible of humility till we never ask to hold the witness of human success in our hands. Entwine thy spirit in our lives to the end that our days may become a clear witness to one supreme gift—the gift of our lives into thy hands. Let the storehouse to thy treasures be opened to us as we trust in thee. Let the bounty of thy love be the witness of our moments and our hours. Thus, O God, deliver us from the danger of human success and make us safe for the glory of thy success, through Jesus Christ our Lord. Amen.

The Seeds of Glory

Read: Philemon 1:1-25

> *"Yes, brother, I want some benefit*
> *from you in the Lord."*
> Philemon 1:20

The seeds of glory are in what we learn to share. From the Damascus Road experience to the prison in Rome, Paul had spent a life of sharing his faith and knowledge of Jesus Christ with all who would receive the message. The twenty-five verses of the short letter to Philemon shine like an iridescent opal amid the cluster of spiritual gems inlaid in the treasury of the New Testament. Paul speaks out of the sharp contrasts of life and thought. Paul, a Roman prisoner, speaks to Philemon, "Yes, brother, I want some benefit from you in the Lord."

Paul is not asking for justice but forgiveness. He is not asking for legal acceptance, but for mercy. Love in its noblest form is being called out in the life of Philemon. And this one great witness from Philemon may well be the pattern for much of our own witnessing for God. Though prisoners to our desires, our prejudices, our loves, we are asked to let the seeds of God's glory become beneficial through our lives.

The achievement of God's glory in human lives is nowhere more pointedly traced than in these words written by Hillyer Straton in *Solving Life's Problems.* "One of the most dramatic instances of the sharing of the religion of Jesus is in the case of a traveling man by the name of L.R. Graves. Years ago he spoke to his friend, Samuel M. Sayford, and kept his name on a private prayer list. Sayford became the secretary of the Evangelistic Association of New England and led C.K. Ober, a student at Williams College, to Christ. In Corness University, Mr. Ober found and influenced John R. Mott, who was struggling over the problem of his lifework. Mott chose Christian service as his career with emphasis on ministry to youth. The result of Mott's choice is endless, for he has influenced more young men and women to choose Christian callings in the world field than any other man. It was a religion that worked for Graves, Sayford, Ober, and Mott."[17] The benefit of sharing was a massive harvest reaped from the lives of these men who let the seeds of God's glory take root and blossom in their lives.

The seeds of glory are God's gift to us. They form the heart-beat of the benefit or witness that God rightly expects of each of us. In the times of our truest sharing we make our most effective witness. Leon Uris, in his novel, *The Exodus,* describes the life of the Jews in the Ghetto. The amazing expression of that dark hour was the high sense of sharing the necessities and the dangers of each moment. There is something within us as it was in Paul, that when he is imprisoned in body, the witness for Christ is unshackled. Paul sees the release of both Philemon and of Onesimus. The glory of God would grow in each of us that we might be free to bear evidence of the divine presence in us. Let the seeds of God's glory work in you that you may be a benefit in the Lord, Jesus Christ.

PRAYER:

Let us meditate upon these words:

> ...and I pray that the sharing of your faith may promote the knowledge of all the good that is ours in Christ.
>
> Philemon 1:6

Lead us, O God, from the imprisonment of our minds, the prejudices of our hearts, the veiled awarenesses of our souls. From the caverns of self-knowledge and the craven places of self-esteem and the hidden valleys of our self-righteousness, deliver us, O God. In the midst of freedom which alone thou canst give, forgive us, our Father, when we are content simply to be free. Freed from our limitations, ensnare us, O Lord, in thy masterful plans. Teach us how to replace the imprisonment of life in self to becoming prisoners of thy love. Let the power of thy forgiveness, mercy, and love reveal through us the light of life for humankind. For thy benefit, O God of hosts, let us in true witness share the faith and knowledge of all the good that is "ours in Christ." Amen.

When We Cannot Win

Read: 2 Corinthians 11:24-29

> *"Who is made to fall, and*
> *I am not indignant?"*
> 2 Corinthians 11:29b

If you think you cannot win, then read this list of Paul's acts in which he failed: "Five times I have received at the hands of the Jews the forty lashes less one. Three times I have been beaten with rods; once I was stoned. Three times I have been ship-wrecked; a night and a day I have been adrift at sea; on frequent journeys, in danger from rivers, danger from robbers, danger from my own people, danger from Gentiles, danger in the city, danger in the wilderness, danger at sea, danger from false brethren; in toil and hardship, through many a sleepless night, in hunger and thirst, often without food, in cold and exposure. And, apart from other things, there is the daily pressure upon me of my anxiety for all the churches" (2 Corinthians 11:24-28). At the conclusion of such a catalog of calamity, we read these masterful words, "Who is weak, and I am not weak? Who is made to fall, and I am not indignant?" (2 Corinthians 11:29). In the midst of such defeating circumstances, Paul's only concern was with those who were trammeled in failure. From a human point of view we would expect the missionary to have some concern for his own hurts. To the contrary, the man of Tarsus thought only of those who had similar failures and bowed to them.

Rudyard Kipling has a point for us to ponder when he writes:

> If you can meet with Triumph and Disaster
> And treat those two imposters just the same.[18]

In success we can be proud, gay, positive. When the glory departs and it seems we have gone down "into the pit," what then? It is time to ask about the *what* and the *why* of life: what we have sought and why we have sought it.

Paul Elmen, in *The Restoration of Meaning to Contemporary Life,* has listed many of the phantom goals of modern living. Not the least of those after which we seek is escape from boredom. Because we are bored with life and because we do not have valid goals for living, not a few seek to fill their lives with all kinds of activities. We immerse ourselves in club and committee meetings, humanitarian deeds, and, at the close of the day, we fall exhausted in a tilt-back chair at home to watch the mediocre offerings of television. Countless are those who forsake their families to become the servants of many and strangers of those who bear their names. For a moment—a few years at most— there is the bright success in these harried lives, like the burst of a three-phase rocket. But, like the rocket, such lives find their orbit in the airless places of space and are unrelated to those who need them most. The *what* of life must be answered, and the Damascus Road convert cast the key into our hands when he declared, "Who is made to fall, and I am not indignant?" If, in the midst of all our failures we are more concerned with those who, like ourselves, suffer, then we have discovered the *what* that can give our lives a vital witness that is true success.

Paul Elmen goes on to point out, "(Man) desperately needs the conviction that he is not alone in the vast, interstellar spaces, and that life has dignity, meaning, and solidity.... He needs glory."[19] The *why* of all our failures must be understood. When we have failed, it is likely we have missed the dignity, meaning, and solidity of life. It may well be we have missed the "glory." The light of God has not gone out, but we have shuttered it from our lives. In this dark moment it remains for us to lament with Shakespeare's Othello:

> If I quench thee, thou flaming minister,
> I can again thy former light restore
> Should I repent me; but once put out thy light,
> Thou cunning'st pattern of excelling nature,
> I know not where is that Promethean heat
> That can thy light relume.[20]

This is a heavy sigh of life, but not its end. Paul could recount the failures. In the midst of it all, he could remain concerned for others who suffered. Finally, his indomitable faith could lead him to say, "I have fought the good fight, I have finished the race, I have kept the faith. Henceforth there is laid up for me the crown of righteousness, which the Lord, the righteous judge, will award to me on that Day, and not only to me but also to all who have loved his appearing" (2 Timothy 4:7-8).

If you think you cannot win, then take heart. When the strength of circumstance would bend your life, stand erect. The glory of God will show you the way through and beyond failure.

PRAYER:

O Lord, try as I will thy light will not come to me. My feet are made of clay, my mind is made only of reason, and my spirit has no wings of faith on which to soar. I need so much. I am so little. The good thoughts are corrupted by cankerous greed. The deed of righteousness is bent to evil by my own selfishness and jealousy. The moment I seek to open my soul to thee, I turn away because my defeats seem easier than to reach for thy glory. To be honest, God, I want to be successful. I want to serve thee, I want to speak thy word and do thy deed. With all my strength and cleverness I have tried. Now I am spent. I can do no more. Lord, take hold of me and do with me and for me what you will. Lord, is it thy glory now I see? Amen.

IV

In Joy and When the Soul Is Crushed

No Secret

Read: Psalm 43

> *"Then I will go to the altar of God,*
> *to God my exceeding joy . . . ."*
> Psalm 43:4a

Many secrets can be hidden in the chambers of the mind. Formulas for strange devices, events of a disquieting past, hopes that linger unfulfilled, even hatreds and loves unexpressed; these are but a few of the secrets closeted in the mind. One secret we cannot keep is the spirit of joy. There is a power about joy that erases lines of sorrow and breaks the face of grief into the smile of confidence. Joy is that spirit which is born deep within the individual and, rising unrepressed, cleanses the entire person as it bursts forth into full light. Even the psalmist in the midst of soul-crushing experiences witnessed to this irrepressible spirit of joy, "Then I will go to the altar of God, to God my exceeding joy...."

Any clear appreciation of the spirit of joy begins with the understanding that, being God's gift to us, it is incapable of being kept secret. Try as we will, we cannot behave as the poet has thought:

> I'll make my Joy a secret thing;
> My face shall wear a mask of care;
> And those who hunt a Joy to death,
> Shall never know what sport is there![21]

To the contrary, Jesus prompts us to present the face of joy to all people at all times, even when we are in the midst of trying circumstances. The thought is expanded as we read, "And when you fast, do not look dismal, like the hypocrites, for they disfigure their faces that their fasting may be seen by men. Truly, I say to you, they have received their reward. But when you fast, anoint your head and wash your face, that your fasting may not be seen by men but by your Father who is in secret; and your Father who sees in secret will reward you" (Matthew 6:16-18). Let the face of joy be seen at all times. It is God's gift to us. When joy is in our hearts it must not, it cannot, be kept a secret.

Joy is more than a spirit that springs from our eyes and lips; it tinctures the deeds of our days. Raymond T. Stamm suggests, "Joy that is the fruit of the Spirit sprang from a life that was gracious and kind, full of good will, generous to impart itself to others, glad when they accepted and rejoiced with it, but forgiving, and still singing, when men rejected and persecuted it."[22] Just as joy is the product of this kind of life, so this manner of witnessing is the product of the spirit of joy that God has indwelt in us. The order of this matter is properly set in the song that youth in church conferences have sung for years, "Joy, Joy, Joy, Joy, Down in My Heart." First in the heart and then expressed in daily deeds, this is the way of God "my exceeding joy."

Fulton Oursler writes of Nannie, a member of the household staff of an English family.[23] Nannie had "implacable cheerfulness" that she expressed in the face of all circumstances. Her sense of joy was expressed in her smile, her words, and her deeds. She transformed the life of the household where she served. Even when she lay critically ill, Nannie knew how to make those smile who shared her ward in the hospital. Her unfailing witness to the joy in her heart was no secret. In the expressing of that joy, Nannie found her own health restored.

What troubles beset you? Set them clearly in your mind. Then read again the words of Psalm 43. Nearly half of this song describes the hurts of life. Then, with the psalmist, search out the joy that God has placed in your heart. Let it leaven your whole being. Rise up from the ash-heap of your grief that the "exceeding joy" of God may speak through you and bring you new life. When joy is a secret it is dead. Let your joy be in your words and your deeds that all may see your witness to the God of "exceeding joy."

PRAYER:

Forgive us, Lord, when the burdens which encumber our lives are written deep in line and deed upon our face and life. O how great is our sin that in all our haste we have sought to embrace tomorrow across the obstacle of today. How deep is our misery when we let the shadows of yesterday blight the happiness which thou hast given us at the beginning of this hour. Make us, Lord, pilgrims and pioneers of today. Let it be sufficient that the joy of thy presence is in us. May the particles of thy presence filter through our entire being. Let the full flood of joy cleanse us of our sin. May men ever see in our face and deed the light of thy glory and give honor to thy name. Amen.

Darkness Prevails

Read: Isaiah 24:4-13

> " . . . all joy has reached its eventide;
> the gladness of the earth is banished."
>
> Isaiah 24:11b

Like a dagger the words of Isaiah penetrate the mind. They describe what all have felt sometime in life. The prophet expresses our unalloyed grief when the soul is crushed:

> All joy has reached its eventide;
> the gladness of the earth is banished.

It is easy for the tired pilgrim and the weary pioneer to feel the mounting tension of human and spiritual hurts that weigh down the wings of the world. The writer of Ecclesiastes has a phrase that aptly expresses this matter when he states, "the sun and the light and the moon and the stars are darkened and the clouds return after the rain" (Ecclesiastes 12:2).

It is not difficult to note a few of the times when soul-crushing darkness prevailed. At the beginning of World War II, the small town of Lidice, Czechoslovakia seemed safely removed from the mainstream of hostility. In June 1942, the entire male population of the town was destroyed in reprisal for the assassination of SS General Reinhard Heydrick. The women were interned in concentration camps where all but a hundred died. Only a handful of the children could be discovered after the war. The population decimated and the village razed, it seemed unlikely Lidice would ever live again. Correspondent Alan Burgess told us that a new settlement was being developed. Out of the soul-crushing experience, life was emerging. To remind the people of the sorrows of Lidice a monument was erected, topped by a cross bearing a crown of barbed wire. This is the story of a thousand places left in the wake of a Genghis Khan, Napoleon, or Hitler. The maps of Lidice, Hiroshima, or Nagasaki can verify the places. In these woeful times and places darkness prevailed and many must have said:

> All joy has reached its eventide;
> the gladness of the earth is banished.

The soul that is crushed by external circumstances is no less hurt than the soul that crouches in darkness because of inner spiritual despair. Dr. Harold C. Urey, the atomic scientist, said, "I am a frightened man." The discovery of atomic energy promised new light to the world, but the man who was responsible for its discovery was frightened at what had been revealed. Alfred Nobel developed dynamite and beheld his new creature to be so destructive as to hold promise to the world that its great destructive power might lead humankind to choose peace. We can all understand the fear of these men because we are their children playing with the toys they gave us. The souls of men pay a crushing tax for their brilliant discoveries, and "all joy" seems to have reached "its eventide."

John Milton reveals the same struggle of the soul crushed beneath the weight of personal tragedy. Grappling with the blindness that beset him, Milton wrote:

> When I consider how my light is spent,
> E're half my days, in this dark world and wide,
> And that one Talent which is death to hide,
> Lodg'd with me useless, though my Soul more bent
> To serve therewith my Maker, and present
> My true account, lest he returning chide,
> Doth God exact day-labor, light deny'd,
>
> I fondly ask; but patience, to prevent
> That murmur, soon replies, God doth not need
> Either man's work or his own gifts, who best
> Bear his mild yoke, they serve him best, his State
> Is Kingly. Thousands at his bidding speed,

And post o'er Land and Ocean without rest:
They also serve who only stand and wait.[24]

When it seems "the gladness of the earth is banished" there remains little else for anyone to do than to "stand and wait." Then, by God's grace, we look both within and without to find the light.

PRAYER:

Here and now, O God, we acknowledge our fears—the times when we believe there is no hope and the fresh breeze of thy presence does not caress our flushed living. The caprice of circumstance we cannot control and the despair which rises from within are the twin demons which seek to cast their dice of fate. Driven by the craven impulse to flee from all we cannot control or understand, O God, we beseech thee, give us the strength to "stand and wait." Keep us from complete desolation, when laughter is stilled and the fountains of joy have withered. Beyond the borders of our knowing, let thy spirit range, and let us be content to stand enshrouded in darkness till thy light appears. As reeds shaken by the storm, so our souls are tossed. Lord, let us not despise the fear, the tossing, or the despair. Though we know not how or why—keep us close to thee, through Christ, our Lord. Amen.

Seen and Unseen

Read: 1 Peter 1:3-9

> *"Without having seen him you love him;*
> *though you do not now see him you*
> *believe in him and rejoice with*
> *unutterable and exalted joy."*
> 1 Peter 1:8

Peter had penetrating insight into things that God meant to man. Christ was no longer in their midst, and some who had become Christians had never seen Christ. Both groups of believers were bound together not because they had seen or had not seen Christ, but because they loved and believed in him and "rejoiced with unutterable and exalted joy." Those who had seen Christ knew the heartache of losing their teacher. Those who had never seen the Master knew the frustration of feasting on divine truth without the benefit of the teacher. These two groups represent the real despair that infiltrates the soul and in the darkness of which it is scarcely possible for us to hold our ground.

Love and belief are the only sparks of light that might be fanned into a beacon flame. Feeble as they are, love and belief are the twin hopes of women and men. They are the seen and the unseen that God sets a-flickering in humankind's most desperate hour. Though the "light went out all over Europe" at the beginning of World War I, the light of hope was not extinguished in human hearts. When Adnoriam Judson was asked about the prospects of converting the people of Burma, he replied, "They are as bright as the promises of God." The poet Wylie saw the witness of our Lord on his way to Calvary in these words:

Weary, sad, alone, I stood at the crest of the world,
While beneath far away stretched
Sea and land to the banners of blue unfurled.
The path I had come seemed too far away for returning

to quiet sod;
From that moment of pain and bright
Agony I climbed hand in hand with God.[25]

In the most vacant moment of human despair, God seeks us out
with the light of love and belief. The love we can see. It lives within
us and we can feel its movements. On the simplest level the love
that brings light is expressed by the psalmist who said, "Weeping
may tarry for the night, but joy comes with the morning" (Psalm
30:5b). There is still a deeper expression of this inward love. Paul
declares the matter to the Christians in Philippi, "Complete my
joy by being of the same mind, having the same love, being in full
accord and of one mind" (Philippians 2:2). Harold Wilke, who
knows the problems of the physically handicapped, suggests that
"the attitudes of one's family and friends" composed one of his
major problems. The handicapped person is "seen first as
handicapped, and only secondly as a person." The spiritually
handicapped—those whose souls are crushed—need to see
themselves as persons. They need to discover the light and love
of God that lives within them. Harold Wilke discovered this truth
and witnesses to it in word and deed in the Christian ministry.
Listen to his words: "Again, healing comes from above. In the
darkest hours of life, man is not alone. There is always the Holy
One beside him. God seems to come easily in joy, yet also in
sorrow we know his presence."[26]

The Christian is called to witness to this love of God and
thereby "rejoice with unutterable and exalted joy." At the same
time, witnessing urges us to know the unseen powers that move
in our behalf. After Jesus' resurrection, he made several appear-
ances to his followers. None is more perfect in its imagery than
when he appeared to his disciples who had returned to their
fishing nets. John's gospel tells it this way: "Simon Peter said to
them, 'I am going fishing.' They said to him, 'We will go with
you.' They went out and got into the boat; but that night they
caught nothing. Just as the day was breaking, Jesus stood on the
beach..." (John 21:3-4a). What an amazing statement—"Just as
the day was breaking, Jesus stood on the beach ...!" It has been
said, "all night Jesus was coming to them." That is what he is
doing for us all the time. He is coming to us when we do not see
him. In the seen presence of love in our lives and in the unseen

51

movements of our Lord, we are undergirded to the end that we may witness for our God in joy and when the soul is crushed.

PRAYER:

O Lord, who openest opportunities all around us, quicken our souls that we may grasp the love and belief that is ever near. In patience we witness unto thee as we "stand and wait." Deliver us from becoming stolid in dumb resignation. Let the feeble sparks of thy love rekindle our hope and set our lives burning after thee. Let the still darkness which makes our eyes and our minds unseeing reveal thy coming unto us. Lord, forgive us when we cast aside love and belief to struggle with the brittle tools of human courage or epic spirit. Let us be quick to increase thy presence with us by our faith in thee. Then, the seen and unseen of thy power will lead us beyond the soul-crushing difficulties of life to rejoicing with thy "unutterable and exalted joy" through Christ our Savior. Amen.

Joy Reborn

Read: Luke 21:10-19

> *"This will be a time for you to bear
> testimony."*
> Luke 21:13

The Christian witness involves every area and mood of life. In joy, in soul-crushing experiences, in rekindling, and in the reemergence of joy, we witness to our love and devotion of God. At this point two interesting qualities of joy become apparent. First, the fact that joy, being the gift of God, is indestructible. Second, the greatest time for us to witness is when joy is reborn.

Joy, like love, is indestructible because it is God's gift to us. Clifford Bax, in poem form, has declared, "All we had of joy endures, a joy within us."[27] Though we have been preoccupied with the distress of external hazard and internal turmoil, joy lives within us. Like some long-lost experience that the psychiatrist seeks to bring to the surface, so joy remains the residue of God within our lives. Joy awaits that proper moment when it can be properly called forth. The seed slumbers within the bosom of the earth awaiting the gentle caress of spring. Joy remains unseen, unnoticed, and untarnished within the soul. It awaits that precious moment when we dare to unclog the spiritual veins of life and let it rush to the surface again.

When Arthur Sullivan's brother died, it seemed the famous composer's world would collapse. Turning to the organ, this man, who had worked with W.S. Gilbert to produce many delightful scores of music, found his hands "wandering idly over the noisy keys." It was as though the pall of sorrow would choke any melody that would seek to speak. From this aimless playing emerged a masterful theme that we know as "The Lost Chord." Adelaide A. Procter caught the mood of the composer when she wrote these words:

Seated one day at the Organ
I was weary and ill at ease,
And my fingers wandered idly
Over the noisy keys.

I know not what I was playing,
Or what I was dreaming then;
But I struck one chord of music,
Like the sound of a great Amen.

Joy is the great Amen of life that is constantly reborn in life. No pall or shroud, no disillusionment or grief can stifle the joy that God has so wondrously woven into the fabric of life. Leaping out of the subconscious comes what William Cullen Bryant has called the "voice of gladness, and a smile of eloquence of beauty." The first great fact for the crushed soul is the consciousness that joy is forever reborn.

The second fact to remember is that the greatest time for us to witness is when joy is reborn. A seminary professor was wont to counsel his students by saying, "No one is fit for the ministry until he has been so tried by his work as to determine to quit the ministry, then finding new strength he decides to remain in his work." The real treasure of joy is to be found in its being reborn.

In the deeps of soul-hurt, let us walk with sandals of faith, awaiting the joy of God that brings again the wreaths of smiles and restores us to our witnessing ways.

PRAYER:

Lord, how good it is to stand on the windswept shores of the ocean. Our cheeks feel the brash rush of wind that catches at cloth and flesh; our eyes behold the fearsome darkness of the storm in all its raging fury; our senses reel before the impact of its terrible might. Lord, though we stand, we tremble. Then with the eye of faith, we know that deep, deep down in the midst of the sea the waters are still. Though we cannot see, we know there is a central calm and peace; and, this serenity must break the surface and bestill the tossing waves. O God, let the parable of the sea be seen as the parable of our lives. Forgive us when we are prisoners of the storm. Deliver to us that sweet assurance that the joy which thou hast given us will rise again. With eagerness of soul, O Lord, we reach out to witness for thee as joy is reborn. Amen.

V

In Health and When the Body Is Stricken

Great Treasure

Read: 1 Corinthians 3:16-23

> *"Do you not know that you are*
> *God's temple and that God's*
> *spirit dwells in you?"*
> 1 Corinthians 3:16

"Health alone is victory." These words of Thomas Carlyle reveal a truth often taken for granted and seldom appreciated. Our Lord made clear the worth of one's physical well-being when he observed, "Those who are well have no need of a physician, but those who are sick" (Mark 2:17b).

Paul states the matter more positively in his letter to the Christians at Corinth, "Do you not know that you are God's temple and that God's Spirit dwells in you?" There is a relationship between our health and the fact that God dwells in us. Surely, this is another of the Eternal's gifts to us. As such, it follows, we are under constraint to use this gift of great treasure for our Lord.

The sure image of God's temple is the person in the fullness of good health. Our physical well-being is a treasure we misuse, as is explained by Helmut Thielicke when he said, "True, everything we have comes from our Father, our ability, our industry, our technical know-how. But when we use it without him, when we treat it as paid-out capital which we can use as we please, it decays in our hands."[28]

In a strange sense our health is not so much the real treasure as the multitude of worthwhile things such health makes possible for each of us to do. The vigor with which a day is spent, the power with which our service is rendered, the inclusiveness of love expressed to each person; these form the valued essences of our treasured health. As a consequence, we can accept this gift of great treasure, and at the same time, use the gift for God's will.

When Jesus wished to describe the inclusive intensity with which we are called upon to witness for God, he said, "and you shall love the Lord your God with all your heart, and with all your soul, and with all your mind, and with all your strength" (Mark 12:30).

Among all the definitions of "strength" must rest the notion that we are to use all of our physical strength (health) to serve God. This is more than a human idea; it is the summation of the law and prophets. It is the gathering of the wisdom of our Lord into a few words.

The "unsunned miser's treasure" is not equal to that which God has given us in the pulse-beat of the body, the power of the lungs, the strength of the arms. These physical elements, fitly united and driven by the power of God indwelling in us, are God's gift and our great treasure without which part of the Divine's purpose will not be properly achieved.

It is in the rainbow days of our health that we must seek out God. The advice of the writer of Ecclesiastes is true, "Remember also your Creator in the days of your youth" (Ecclesiastes 12:1a). The great treasure of health is fleeting at best and it is that moment when we prepare for that which is yet to come. Those who are able to witness in health find it a joy to bear testimony of their faith when the vestige of health has departed. The stories of David march in giant strides across the pages of the Old Testament. In the power of his youth, he loved and served God. As a result, his latter days magnified the Lord and made him a man of wisdom. Dr. Thomas Dooley served God in the power of his treasured youth, and he continues to serve as contemporary youth accept his life as an ideal.

In still another sense, the treasure of health provides us the opportunity to prepare for our own times when the body is stricken. A prominent cancer physician in the Midwest has said, "The time to prepare for cancer is when you are healthy." He went on to say, "When I lecture it is to explain that one out of four will have cancer and the time to prepare for cancer is when you do not have it." You may think this morbid. But the certainty of illness and death must be faced. The best time to prepare for death is when we are strong. A minister, lecturing to a group of physicians and ministers, declared, "The people who are most afraid of death are those who are healthy. For the most part, those who are dying do not fear death." Our health is a gift of God, a vital time of bearing our witness for God, a time for storing up the treasures of good living, a time for preparing for those days when the body is stricken.

PRAYER:

How unthinking we have been, O Lord. At birth we could not know and in childhood we understood only vaguely the majesty of thy gift to us in the strength and health of our bodies. Even in our youth, we have squandered what we thought was our own. Later we spent in abandon the treasure of our health to gain a treasure which "moth and rust corrupt." Still, O God, our feverish lives. Teach us how to pause and give thanks for our day of health and strength. Reveal to us that this is thy gift of human bounty to be used to bear our faith in thee. Then, O Lord, lead us to use our health to prepare for that future when the body is stricken and our witness for thee must be climaxed. Lord, let our days be precious jewels of gathered treasure which will adore thee. Amen.

Cloudy Skies

Read: Lamentations 3:40-48

"*. . .thou hast wrapped thyself with a cloud*
so that no prayer can pass through."
Lamentations 3:44

Dr. Brewster Higley wrote for us to sing,

Where seldom is heard a discouraging word
and the skies are not cloudy all day.

But the skies are cloudy some days. The writer of Lamentations knew the clouds of bondage in a far country. He wrote graphically of the tragic despair that seeps into the heart and encases the mind in the muck of despondency. In our modern living, we have been successful in pushing aside much of the physical illness that once made the days of many a blistering storm of searing pain. Dr. K.R. Eissler reminds us, however, that "Science has not come closer to eliminating death but has only combatted death by postponement."[29] The cloudy days are sure to come. In health

59

we have the opportunity to prepare for the darker times by increasing faith, husbanding our physical strength, and filling the storehouse of the mind with good thoughts.

Sometimes the clouds come in filmy form hardly noticeable to the eye of the mind. Almost as pestering nuisances, the power of health is bleached away. These are the common difficulties that beset us all and that belabor our days with excuses. There is a legend at Harvard that the late LeBaron Russell Briggs, beloved dean of the college, once asked a student why he had failed to complete an assignment. "I wasn't feeling very well, sir," said the student. "Mr. Smith," said the dean, "I think that in time you may perhaps find that most of the work of the world is done by people who aren't feeling very well." The haze of "not feeling well" has misled many a person into defeat, while others with much more serious maladies have fought on through thickening storm to bear their witness. It is this latter circumstance that more properly demands our attention. Casting aside our temporary hindrances to comfort, we do our tasks. But, when the real storm clouds appear, we move into deeper contemplations. It is here that doubt, fear, and uncertainty form the heavy clouds that lay rigid bands of spiritual mummification on our days.

Doubt is the most deadening of all human foes. It saps the spiritual vitality because one is, in this state, incapable of staying with the past or reaching to the future. The present seems an intolerable state of vacillation that has neither beginning nor end. What has been cannot be recaptured and what is to be seems unbearable. This very thing that is in the present seems impossible to accept. So it is with the individual who believes he has a malignancy living within his body. The joy of the past cannot be reborn and the prospects of the future seem unreal. Even the present promises no hope. The beginning of real hope in this cloud that debilitates us in its awesome tentacles is the knowledge of fact. Virginia Nichols, a missionary in South Africa, describes her battle with doubt: "When I first heard the news, (that she had cancer) I felt it was sad—from my point of view—to depart when there were twenty-six more years of service before I would come to my natural retirement. Later on, I began to see that this problem is no problem for a Christian. When I faced up to it in 1957, I realized that it must be faced completely ... it is much better to face it once and for all." Every minister and physician knows that doubt is one of the deadliest of human enemies. To know the worst seems to release the soul from its cloud of utter frustration and the power of faith and prayer begin to open the silt-filled channels of the soul. Knowledge is the beginning of hope when the clouds of physical distress form.

Fear is the close companion of doubt. As flowers grow in rich soil, so doubt is the compost of fear. There is fear of that which we do not know or cannot understand. There is a cold fear that pain will become relentless suffering. There is fear that we will not be able to face these challenges with clear minds and courageous hearts. In the quieter moments of meditation, the soul must turn from "fear" to the spiritual entities that can overcome our awful state. We have all read from the Psalm, "The Lord is my Shepherd," but we have not always contemplated what it means to behave like sheep. The Gospel of John gives us a clear statement of the place of the shepherd: "and he calls his own sheep by name and leads them out. When he has brought out all his own, he goes before them, and the sheep follow him"(John 10:3b-4a). The condition of the sheep is to learn how to follow. And, they will discover:

> God has not promised skies always blue,
> Flower-strewn pathways all our lives through;
> . . . .
> But God hath promised strength for the day,
> Rest for the labor, light for the way.

The first step in conquering fear is the knowledge that we are God's sheep. The next step is to seek out the meaning in our fear. Could it be that pain has something to offer us? Our age does not want to suffer though it has known much of human hurt. The unknown poet meditated on these words and has given us this wisdom:

> The cry of man's anguish went up to God
> Lord take away the pain!
> . . . .
> Then answered the Lord to the cry of the world,
> Shall I take away pain,

61

And with it the power of the soul to endure
Made strong by the strain?
Shall I take away pity that knits heart to heart
And sacrifice high?
Will ye lose all your heroes that lift from the fire
White brows to the sky?
Shall I take away love that redeems with a price
And smiles at its loss?
Can ye spare from your lives that would cling unto Mine
The Christ on His Cross?

A major who had served long in the cause of Christ in the Salvation Army discovered he was dying of cancer. Despite the deep clouds of pain he was able to say, "Only those with great spiritual blessings does God entrust with cancer." Search out the blessings that may well be yours as the clouds begin to form. Fear can drive us to craven shame or it can be the doorway that opens upon the approaches of a nobler faith. Despise not the cloud of fear or doubt, but love more the prospects to which they can lead.

The final dissolution of many comes in the form of uncertainty. The promptings of disease seem to cut off any sense of the future. The uneven present gives no assurance of immediate stability. Consequently, doubt and fear mingle to produce a state of complete uncertainty.

The only hope in such a state is the gathering of the truth based upon facts. Uncertainty is that final cloud in which the human soul is lost and out of which "no prayer can pass." When sure knowledge of the nature and diagnosis of physical illness has been established, then the soul is able to meet the challenge. The passage through uncertainty is not often discovered in the spoken word. Rather it is a growing awareness of the real condition of the body. Simultaneously the soul stirs itself to a higher attainment of vitality. As the body decreases, the spirit increases. Finally, the spiritual dominates life and the person is able to penetrate with prayer the clouds of fear, doubt, and uncertainty.

Lamentation is a reasonable part of life. It is not designed to keep us in a trough of despair, but to lead us to a nobler spiritual vitality. Let us seek the power of the spirit to penetrate and dissipate the clouds of despair.

PRAYER:

Thank you, God, for all the days when the skies of my life have been bright with radiant sunshine and o'er-cast with the peerless blue of the sky. My heart rejoices that the whole of nature has rejoiced with me. Now in the dust of the gathering storm, my heart falters, my eyes are dim, my soul is disquieted in me. In this troubled moment, I see the flowers nestled in the bed of protective grass, I know the birds have taken refuge in their nests set in the nook of the trees' arms. Thou hast taken thought of the "flowers of the field" and the "birds of the air." Surely, O Lord, thou wilt show me the way through and beyond the clouds of despair. I know not what tomorrow has in store for me. I am content to know that thy spirit will be with me then as it has been in the past and is with me now. In this great assurance of thy holy presence, O Lord, renew, restore, and keep me. O, let my prayers pierce the clouds of doubt, fear, and uncertainty, and let me stand humbly in thy presence. My soul is open to you, O God, through the loving mercy of our Lord, Jesus Christ. Amen.

Bad News

Read: Psalm 112

> *"He is not afraid of evil tidings;*
> *his heart is firm, trusting in the LORD."*
> Psalm 112:7

In a communication-conscious age, good and bad news are mingled on the front page of each newspaper. The reporters of radio and the commentators on television convey the pleasing and the unsatisfactory accounts of life into our living rooms. We find it impossible to escape this bombardment every day in the year. We rejoice with the good reports and we are saddened with the bad news. In the midst of this vast interplay of fact and emotion there comes that one particular day when we receive bad news that applies to us personally. In all likelihood, we have been growing aware of the message before we heard it.

Bad news is not broken by kind tactful word.
The message is spoken ere the word can be heard.
The eye and the bearing, the breath make it clear,
And the heart is despairing before the ears hear.[30]

We suspect with the heart before the ears hear. Try as we will, we find it impossible to beat back the deeper movements of our consciousness. When the word is spoken, it is harsh but not unexpected. Although we may not have anticipated the word, when it does come we are smitten as a dry leaf caught in the autumn whirlwind. The mind reels, the body goes weak, and the senses numb. The soul seems to be withered like a cactus crumpled on the desert floor. This is our state when bad news overtakes us and we learn that the body is stricken.

Unless we overcome this first shock there can be no hope. Surely, bad news cannot be changed into good news. The fact is clear. But bad news may make it possible for us to see the good or to overcome the bad with a deeper consciousness of the soul. Some disabilities of the body may limit life and, in reality, benefit life. Diminished eyesight can lead us to read more carefully and selectively thereby profiting our mental and spiritual content. Diabetes often provides the patient with the opportunity of caring for the body through diet and in a manner so as to prolong the years of one's life. Blindness never prevented John Milton from giving the world great poetry. Wilberforce never allowed a hunchbacked body to prevent him from shouldering the burden of leading England to abolish the slave traffic. The first reaction after the cold wave of shock is to see what is left in life and how to use it to witness for God. The second is to see how we can witness for God when the worst is immediately before us.

Sometimes we must bear good news in the worst of circumstances. Such an event is based on the fact that we have the good news with us. The time to prepare for bad news is when we have the freshness of good things all around us. Then, when dark helplessness descends, we have a reservoir of strength from which to draw. Generally, this storehouse of strength is developed because we have given our days to something greater than ourselves. An officer in the Salvation Army shared this experience, which aptly portrays the secret of power in witness. A young lady from Indiana had gone to India in the early days of the mission movement. Cautioned against infection of leprosy, she was determined to minister to the lepers with all her heart and strength. When it was discovered she had leprosy and she was informed that she could not return home, her joy knew no bounds. Her immediate reply was, "Thank God, now I will not have to leave these people." She continued, "There is no longer any reason why I should worry about having to return home. I need not leave these who need me." Bad news does not have to end in blank despair when we have given our days in witness to God. Now, in the midst of untimely circumstances, we can witness for our faith.

Bad news can reveal to us the privilege of new thoughts. Day after day, we are tortured by the numbing routine of caring for immediate needs. The race for security, the marathon of prestige, the tournament of success, all sap our vision and vitality. Beyond the first cold shock of terror comes the flood of new thoughts. The objectives of life are suddenly altered. Mrs. Masters grasped this new trend of thought. Her body was under the pall of cancer and her days had become few in earth-life. During a visit with her minister, she asked, "If I become impatient with my pain, would it be proper to ask God to take me home?" To this question revealing new thought, the pastor answered, "When you were a small child your parents frequently took you visiting. As the hour grew late and your body tired, you would ask your father to take you home. Now, your body grows tired again and with the same confidence that you once spoke to your earthly father, you should ask your heavenly Father to take you home." Life gathers new importance and our lives new perspective. Turn not aside from these new challenges that shall be as revealing and refreshing as any that have ever confronted your life. News may be bad and you may be hurt, but the "everlasting arms" of God both cradle and lead you. Trust God to lead you now for in him we are "not afraid of evil tidings."

PRAYER:

Today, O Lord, I had bad news. I confess my sense of defeat and utter helplessness. The past has lost much of its meaning, the present is a confined torture, and the future promises no apparent hope. In my mind is no clear thought and in my soul the flame has sunk to a flicker. Fan, O God, that faint hope within my spirit. Restore me in my rightful mind. Lead me by thy gracious hand. Let the strength of good things from the past give me purpose. O God, let the might of thy guiding spirit lead me in the future. Reveal to me how I may serve in the midst of my limitation and witness for thee in the depths of my confusion. Most of all, Lord, I do not ask for deliverance from my plight of body, but understanding and faith in my condition. Take thou my feeble hand and let thy strength move through me to witness unto thyself. Amen.

Hope

Read: Romans 4:16-25

"In hope he believed against hope . . . ."
Romans 4:18

"Hope against hope, and ask till you receive." No light shines brighter upon the darkened horizon of life than the stimulus to hope. Bad news comes with its withering blight. Within oneself there is not the strength to overcome its shroud. Only the God-given gift of hope can pull aside the veil and place our feet on sure ground. This is the task that faces each of us when we dare to witness for our Lord. We do not give our evidence alone, but the testimony of God must come through us.

Abraham was one who "in hope...believed against hope." There was no help in the world of nature. No material evidence could avow to the fulfillment of the promise, "I have made you the father of many nations" (Romans 4:17b). When the authority of nature is destroyed, no one is bereft save only those who have no greater hope. The real thrust of our witness is not in the reading of signs visible to the eye, but to trust the promises of divine power. To some this is faith and to all it is hope that has a deeper grounding than apparent knowledge. Abraham hoped not with the laws of nature, but with the promises of God.

As the shock of bad news holds us in its cold grasp, it becomes evident we cannot rely upon knowledge of nature. We are driven from the ramparts of this world to seek the deeper faith through and in which life takes on a fuller, richer meaning. Probing in the deeper recesses of the soul one can discover the reasons for hope that, like the sun, chases the clouds away. The first stirrings of such hope come from the recovery of old truths once held and more recently forgotten. Then comes an awareness that the very disease that threatens the body may well be a new window for a larger vision. Finally, hope rises to its height in the understanding that all is not lost and that much is to be accomplished now and in the future.

Old truths are like treasures buried in a field. Forgotten for years, they gain a resplendent glory when rediscovered in the time of need. Turn the pages of your treasure store. Are not these some of the sources of your buried treasure that now will lead you from bleak despair to a renewed hope?

> Blessed is the man who trusts in the LORD,
>   whose trust is the LORD
> He is like a tree planted by water,
>   that sends out its roots by the stream,
> and does not fear when heat comes,
>   for its leaves remain green,
> and is not anxious in the year of drought,
>   for it does not cease to bear fruit.
> Jeremiah 17:7-8

> The LORD is my shepherd, I shall not want.
> Psalm 23:1

> The LORD is my light and my salvation;
>   whom shall I fear?
> The LORD is the stronghold of my life;
>   of whom shall I be afraid?
> Psalm 27:1

> What is my strength, that I should wait?
>   And what is my end, that I should be patient?

Is my strength the strength of stones,
  or is my flesh bronze?
In truth I have no help in me,
  and any resource is driven from me.

Job 6:11-13

Peace be with you. As the Father has sent me,
even so I send you.

John 20:21

Your treasures may not be in the Scriptures. Perhaps they are in some half-remembered word of song or bit of poetry or moving passage of prose. Search your mind again and again. Let those words of hope rise within you. They are in the storehouse of the mind waiting for your call. And from these the moving power of God will help you fashion a renewed hope for your moments of hurt.

In a closer grip with your distress, hope may well spring from the very disease that fastens itself upon your life. Those who have cancer are frequently aware of a new dimension of life. K.R. Eissler observes, "A cancerous growth creates the imagery of a disease which relentlessly and progressively devours the patient from inside, whereas a heart disease apparently gives the feeling of a chronic state which will be discontinued eventually, but by accidental complications rather than as the result of a merciless course."[31] In a slightly different manner, a prominent physician who deals entirely with cancer patients has said, "There is something blessed about cancer. It gives a calmness to the patient which is not apparent to the same high degree in patients with other diseases."[32] Take a clear, long look at the disease. Face it squarely. In this there is hope.

This is the kind of hope that is based upon searching the deep recesses of God's majestic gift of life. And disease is a part of life as we know it. We may strike out blindly at our obvious hurt and limitation. In such a human reaction, we betray the deeper possibilities of spiritual witness for our faith. Then there are some who would seek to use faith to gain their own ends in some kind of spontaneous cure. This is no time to be testing God or to rebel against the real hope that is possible. Faith is not getting God to do something for us. Faith is learning how to do something in understanding with God. And it may well be that our frantic search for earth-life is but a larger rejection of our witness to the power and intent of eternal life.

Hope belongs to those who dare to witness to their trust in God and seek to come to close grips with their disease. Such hope leads us to see the deeper implications of a nobler spiritual way of life.

At last we find the real maturity of hope in the fact that not all is lost. There remains much for us to accomplish. Centuries before Christ, a man named Socrates was condemned to die. Though escape was made possible, he chose to face death. In the fullness of his philosophical conscience, he drank the cup of hemlock and lay down in peace. Our Lord could have escaped the cross, but he refused any release. It must be noted that 20 percent of the Gospel of Luke deals with this portion of Jesus' life. Read through these pages and see what Christianity would have lost if Christ had not accepted the cross. Indeed, we would have lost the message and the Christ.

Some years ago a member of the church raised this problem when she said, "I have lived more than eighty years. Now I am only a care to my children. Why is it I cannot die?" In reply, someone once wrote, "Would you deprive your children of learning how to express their love to you? When they were small, you loved and cared for them. Do not deprive them of such a great opportunity." Patience in the face of our difficulty is part of our noble witness.

Another form of our witness is to engage in active and worthwhile pursuits. One physician relates the story of a man who worked on the assembly line of an auto manufacturer. The man was stricken with leukemia. Determined to work as long as possible, this man carried on his labors until three days before he died. Robert Louis Stevenson wrote some of his finest literature when he was dying of tuberculosis. Lou Gehrig, famous baseball hero of the New York Yankees, played his favorite game until his body would no longer carry him.

Rainbows do not come in clear weather. It is in the midst of the storm when the sun breaks through the clouds that the rainbow is formed. The glories of life do not come in clear weather. When the storm clouds of bad news have descended, we must seek the sunlight of hope. Then will the soul start up and

69

soar; yes, hope against hope. This is the secret door that leads to the beautiful witness of a rainbow-clad life.

PRAYER:

Thou, alone, Lord, knowest the sleepless nights and the days when the mind would not leave my secret thoughts alone. Thou knowest the fear that has prompted me, the doubt and half-truths which have rolled over me like a mighty sea. Thou hast seen my hope vanish like a rose burned with the frost. Now I understand that this was the nightmare before the dawning. My hope is gone and thy hope has been renewed within me. I light my heart in raptured gratitude that thou hast led me safely on. The first dreadful suspicions and the fearful turmoil of cardinal knowledge are like slumbering giants. Thy presence shades all and assurance is beginning to flow in me. O God, let me not falter again. Let this time of struggle with disease become another of the glories to which my life may witness of thy power and to thy eternal honor. Amen.

Helping Hands

Read: Romans 8:26-27

> *"Likewise the Spirit helps us in our weakness . . . ."*
> Romans 8:26a

Julius Caesar, in a vain attempt to swim the Tiber, cried out to his youthful friend, "Help me, Cassius, or I sink."[33] In the fourteenth chapter of Matthew we read, "And Peter answered him, 'Lord, if it is you, bid me come to you on the water.' He said, 'Come.' So Peter got out of the boat and walked on the water and came to Jesus; but when he saw the wind, he was afraid, and beginning to sink he cried out, 'Lord, save me'"(Matthew 14: 28-

30). "Help me" and "Lord, save me" are the cries of our hearts. We have been self-contained in the easier moments of life. Now that we see the wind rising, we cry out for help.

Paul understands this same human problem when he declares to the Romans, "Likewise the Spirit helps us in our weakness." When our bodies are weak, the senses benumbed, and the future uncertain, we need the power of helping hands. It is comforting to know that God, hearing our pleas, will answer. At the very beginning we must be assured that the Spirit of God is with us. The intensity of the Divine identity with us is given clear expression in Paul's words, "The Spirit himself intercedes for us with sighs too deep for words" (Romans 8:26b). God is with us not so much in the spoken word as in the very breath of the soul that emerges in the midst of our trouble. We have understood God's presence when the body was strong and healthy. It is more important that we know God is with us now. Never before has the promise of our Lord meant so much as when we hear him saying, "I am with you always, to the close of the age" (Matthew 28:20b).

Beyond the promise of God to be "with us" there are other helping hands. In a real sense they are a part of the eternal pattern of our Lord who will not leave us alone. Let us review for our strength these many helping hands.

The doctor—We depend upon the doctor to diagnose our disease, to explain to us our needs, and to give us hope. These are important requirements for our daily living. We would be more firmly strengthened if we knew that many doctors join with one of their number who declared, "My life is brought to bear witness for God. I have felt that, if God had a place for me, I had a mission." The physician went on to observe, "The doctor can incise the flesh, only God can heal the flesh. This describes the power and limitations of the physician." Here is a helping hand springing out of deep spiritual convictions and designed to bring the best of human knowledge and science to bear upon our needs.

The nurse—The labor of the nurse must always bear something of the witness of Florence Nightingale who ministered to the wounded in the Crimean War. The gentle ministry of this woman is in the soothing touch of each nurse's care. Too, there is the strong witness of a Clara Barton who would forsake her clerk's position to tend the wounded in the Civil War. Her

71

determination and dogged persistence is evidenced in each nurse who patiently stays with us in all circumstances.

The family—These are the familiar faces who would share our hurts and cannot. They do share our spiritual struggles and minister to us in the full witness of their faith to express mercy, gentleness, and kindness. It is here that heart leans upon heart. We are grateful for these even when they do not understand our moments of sorrow or when they endeavor to do the impossible of sharing our hurt.

The friends—These are the kindly ones who bring joy to us because they remember. They bring a kind word, a small remembrance in the beauty of a flower. Just to see their faces or to see them standing close by is a source of hope. It is enough to know that someone cares about us. One of our greatest needs is to know we are part of a fellowship that remembers us.

The minister—Another of the helping hands, the minister comes to represent the redeeming mercy and comforting grace of our Lord, Jesus Christ. She opens the clogged passages of the soul and we see God more clearly. We appreciate the genuine "miracle of healing" and, above all, the greater miracle of inner peace because we "trust in the Lord." In sharing the Word of God, through the wonder of prayer, and in the very presence of himself, the minister fills the "supportive role" that our lives so desperately need.

The church—The church is a helping hand in two ways. First, we see it in our memory. It is a place of prayer, anthem, and spiritual renewal. It is a fellowship of seeking persons. It is a hallowed place of sacred memories for our own lives and our loved ones. Finally, the church is a helping hand in that the members of the "beloved fellowship" come to us to share their faith and fellowship. Their regular visits give us a feeling of "belonging" to a group that cares about us.

God does hear our cry, "Lord, save me." He has surrounded us with a host of answers to our pleas. The sighing of our spirit has been transformed into a firm rejoicing that God has remembered us, even us.

"Likewise the Spirit helps us in our weakness...." For some it will mean the renewal of the body in health. For all it will mean the renewal of the soul in the mighty movement of God's Spirit and the precious opportunity to witness to the power of this faith that stills the tempest of the soul and sets glowing the spirit of God that gives our lives eternal purpose.

PRAYER:

Lord, let me recount the circumstances which have brought me to this day. I have come from doubt and fear to understanding. I have known the sharp torture of blind despair and depression. The utter blankness of my days and the desolation of the future seemed too great for me to bear. In such a time the light of hope began to glimmer and rise into full glow. I was surrounded by those who cared for me. The image of thy presence walked in each of those who cared for and ministered to me. Suddenly I realized that my prayers were being answered. Lord, my heart pours itself out in praise to thee for the magnitude of thy blessings. In the uneven ways of life, thy spirit comes not to smooth the way, but to walk with me. Thank you, God, for walking with me and letting me know that thy "everlasting arms" are ever eager to lift me up. Amen.

Solid Assurance

Read: Acts 17:22-31

> *"In him we live and move and*
> *have our being . . . ."*
> Acts 17:28

We do not have to live in Athens to lose contact with God. Paul knew that the people of Athens were a "religious" people. In the midst of their profusion of temples, statues, and relics, they had lost touch with the very Spirit of God. We, like those in Athens, can lose our connection with the Divine.

Such a loss is not to be despised no matter how great the resultant torment of the soul. In this bleak condition where the sinews of faith have been tried and the pattern of hope has been shattered, we find that an ebb tide of strength running away can return in a more abundant form with the flood of newfound hope. The height of solid assurance rediscovered is established in the language of Paul, when he said, "In him we live and move and have our being."

We have discovered the witness of our faith to the honor of God passes through difficult times. In health and in the distortions of sickness, we have discovered something of what it means to give the testimony of our spiritual vitality. Some of us have recovered from our illness and discovered the future holds further expression of physical health. Surely, the opportunities for our witness may be tried, but we have found solid footing. Some of us will not recover, but we have made clear the fashion of our witness, and we know the future is still bright with God's eternal hope. In either event, we have learned to trust God and we are ready to express our faith in God under all circumstances. This is the solid assurance we all need. It is this very confidence born of God that alters our present and highlights our future.

The assurance that is ours takes varied forms according to our particular conditions. One expression comes through transformed life in health after sickness. A prominent man in a midwestern village discovered this fact for himself. Driven by a desire to be successful in the world of politics and finance, he had forgotten the importance of persons for the joy of possessing things. In the crucible of suffering, he saw the bright witness of those whose lives formed the helping hands to his dark distress. So transformed was this man by the witness of others and the rebirth of the Spirit of God within his life, that he became the most loved man in the community. Selfishness was replaced with generosity, greed with love, and getting with giving. The passage from health to sickness and back to health was a spiritual transformation. Now, this man witnesses to the substantial fact that "In Him we live and move and have our being." His life is a strong witness based upon solid assurance of God's vital presence.

Assurance may spring up in the midst of our sickness to give us achievement above what we ever hoped to be possible. The experience of Thomas Mann, famous German author, is a vivid point in this matter. The author was working on his novel *Doktor Faustus*. The specter of death was before him. In the midst of this work the possibility of death vanished and the nature of the work changed. Let K.R. Eissler tell it in his own words: "The report (Mann, 1949) as it stands now is in parts a magnificent work, moving at times—in my estimation—to the heights of Tolstoy's *The Death of Ivan Ilyitch*. Yet the tragic height of the work is suddenly interrupted when the author reached the point where he is admitted to a modern hospital. Then the mystery of death vanishes under the impact of the array of technological paraphernalia. The immensity of death which pervades the preceding pages is suddenly reduced to the dimension of a simple industrial process. The tension differential between the two parts symbolizes very well what might happen to great art when the reality of death is conjured away by the reassurances of scientific therapy."[34]

The possibility of death provides its own assurances. The mind drives on, the spirit gathers and marshalls its powers, the body is ready to give us its last neap tide of strength. All of this is possible that we may make that one vital witness for which we have lived. It is as though, in complete self-abandonment, we live and move and have our being in God. This is another form of the solid assurance that is ours.

At last there is the solid assurance that belongs to those who know they will not recover. The need to be witnesses for God is just as great for them as for anyone. In the gathering gray mists of life that is becoming Life, the power of our witness must declare itself.

One of the grandest testimonies we can exhibit is not unlike that made by a lady who had suffered long with a malignancy. A few days before her death, she declared, "My body will soon be at rest and there will be no more pain." Russell Dicks has said that the words *At Rest* engraved on his mother's casket gave him profound comfort. It is solid assurance to know that this is something to which we can witness and of which God gives us because we "live and move and have our being" in him.

Each of us has difficulty in knowing how best to express our faith in God. At the beginning and at the last let it be always to tell all, "In him we live and move and have our being...."

PRAYER:

Thy unfailing spirit has led us, O Lord, amid the trials of every circumstance. When we lost you in the grayness of human hurt, thou didst stand beside us and ministered through human hands. Thy soothing spirit sank deep within our troubled souls. In the strong days when health returned, thy spirit did not forsake us. Thou didst guide us to fashion a new life and sustain a new witness. Even when we testified in thy behalf in the former times of strength, thy presence prepared us for this new way of life. Thou didst not forsake us when life became limited and the future uncertain. With the quickness of light, thou hast set a new warmth in our souls. We know "we cannot drift beyond thy love and care." And it is enough to know we are in thy holy care. In health or sickness, in weakness or in strength, O Lord, keep us close to thee. And in ever-living contact with thy spirit let our thoughts, words, and deeds bear the evidence of our trust in thee, through Jesus Christ, our Lord. Amen.

VI

In Righteousness and When the Moral Ties Are Broken

Self-righteousness

Read: Matthew 5:17-20

". . . unless your righteousness exceeds that
of the scribes and Pharisees, you will
never enter the kingdom of heaven."
Matthew 5:20b

On the way to the tree of life, God has set a "flaming sword which turned every way..."(Genesis 3:24b). Across the pathway that leads to God, there stands a flaming word: "unless your righteousness exceeds that of the scribes and Pharisees, you will never enter the kingdom of heaven." Our Lord did not describe the scribes and Pharisees as being unrighteous. He did call for us to have a righteousness that exceeds theirs.

Our modern use of the word *righteousness* does not allow us the real savor of its meaning. The word seems to describe a form or technique. If, somehow, we can learn to perform the proper deeds in the accepted manner, we will develop righteousness. Unfortunately, we do not see the word as it was written in early English. In Chaucer it was called "right-wis-ness." It was a matter of right wisdom in the sense of being wise in the understanding and practice of things that are good and true. The scribes had righteousness as we understand it; Jesus asked them to have "right-wis-ness." In the tension between these two meanings toil many lives. The scribes and Pharisees hardened into a brittle self-righteousness. Jesus called for an organism of right wisdom and conduct. In the conflict between these concepts of life-conduct each of us lifts our witness to God.

Jesus describes the peril of self-righteousness in vivid terms according to the writing of Luke: "Two men went up into the temple to pray, one a Pharisee and the other a tax collector. The Pharisee stood and prayed thus with himself, 'God, I thank thee that I am not like other men, extortioners, unjust, adulterers, or even like this tax collector. I fast twice a week, I give tithes of all that I get'"(Luke 18:10-12). Aside from the fact that the Pharisee was describing a mechanical type of religion in listing the things he did, the real core of this statement is seen in the few words often overlooked, "The Pharisee stood and prayed thus with himself...." Self-righteousness sweeps God from the cosmos and from the human mind. In the vacancy that results, the human form begins to grow like some grotesque form of nocturnal dream. Distorted beyond all imagination, we place our own tumid image in the chancel of the heart. The result? We pray to ourselves. The best we can offer God is the cellophane-wrapped gifts of our assembly-line faith.

This diabolical power of self-righteousness is ever close to each of us. The apostle Peter was very close to this human form of witness when Jesus sought to wash his feet. You will recall Peter first refused such humble service. Unable to reject the Christ, then Peter said, "Lord, not my feet only but also my hands and my head!" (John 13:9b). Peter's self-righteousness sought to dominate the will of God expressed through this humble deed of our Master.

We are asked to witness for Christ in righteousness and not in self-righteousness that leads us to "pray with ourselves," or to list our credentials of good deeds, or strive to dominate the will of God with our own will. Our righteousness must exceed that of the scribes and Pharisees.

The kind of righteousness to and in which we are called to witness is a gift of God. While our witness is dependent in part upon our learning of the will of our heavenly Father, it is more largely a matter of keeping our lives open to the movement of the Divine Spirit. The multiplication tables are a part of knowledge because they can be taught. Righteousness is not knowledge but the use of wisdom. This is something that comes to those whose souls are open to the "will of God." Amos, the shepherd of Tekoa, had wisdom because he sought after God. Jeremiah, that learned man of the city, had wisdom because he sought the counsel of the Lord. Jesus had wisdom because he let his soul leap beyond the limitation of learning to walk in the valley and hillcrest with God. Francis of Assisi had wisdom because he spent hours in meditation and prayer opening his soul-chambers to the incoming Spirit of the Eternal. Abraham Lincoln had wisdom that flowed in his words at Gettysburg because he had often been upon his knees in prayer.

We are called to witness for God who is a spirit. When we try to reduce the message of the Lord to textbook form, or to list it in the "body of the law," or to catalog it in the form of good deeds, we lift only the empty shell of learning in the form of self-righteousness. When we give evidence of right-wis-ness, we have long been on the hardboards of prayer to rise and walk in the green pastures of divine wisdom. It is here we have celestial company and engage a witness that marks us as "sons of God."

PRAYER;
Lord of righteousness, lead us, we beseech thee, in the ways of thy wisdom. Purge from our souls each thrust of our self-righteousness. Cleanse our minds of thoughts which crowd out thy image and magnify our sense of self-importance. Free our hands from slavish devotion to doing only deeds of self-righteousness. Deliver our lips from recounting the events of a religion constructed from the erector-set of human knowledge. Lord, let our souls stand open and free to thy every moving impulse. Let us speak thy wisdom, carry the message of thy love in deed both beautiful and free, and discover our souls captained by thy eternal purposes. Give us, we ask, the wisdom of thy presence which is not less than truth divine and a life of witness which is thy kingdom within us. Amen.

Running Away

Read: Luke 15:11-24

> *". . . (he) gathered all he had and took his*
> *journey into a far country . . . ."*
> Luke 15:13b

Have you ever run away from home? *The Adventures of Huckleberry Finn* by Mark Twain tells of just such experiences. Those who have never engaged in this adolescent adventure may well have anticipated possible joys from such experiments. Whether we run away from home or not it must be noted that not a few do run away from what home means. Running away from home may be more than a temporary escapade; it may be a witness to that against which we rebel. We are seeking escape. We would be as Henry Bunner describes in his lines:

Happy the mortal free and independent,
Master of the mainspring of his own volition!

How is it we do not discern the real lament that must
inevitably come as the poet goes on to observe,

Look on us with the eye of sweet compassion:
We are Cook's Tourists.[35]

The young son in the parable of the prodigal son gathered
together his possessions and ran away into a "far country." No
one had ever told him—or if they did he did not understand—that
he carried with him to the far country more than he knew. His
baggage consisted of the things that were his. Just so! His
clothing, his wealth, and most of all, his hopes, fears, desires, and
dreams. For good and for evil, he took with him all of his
possessions.

It is this very fact that causes the moral ties of life to be broken.
We witness to our inability to understand that we do not escape
what we are or the background from which we have sprung. A
young mother expressed this matter vividly when she sobbed out
her story to her minister. "I ran away to get married. I know now
I was not in love with the man I married. I was trying to run away
from my parents, my sister who seemed to have things better
than I, and from the disreputable condition of the house we called
a home." Unfortunately, this young lady took with her all that she
possessed. She ran away only to discover that all she had left was
still with her.

Not long ago the pastor of a large urban congregation
revealed another type of our witness to running away. A young
man came with his fiancée to make arrangements for their
marriage. The wedding was necessary because of the pregnancy
of the girl. In careful counseling it was discovered that both these
young people were running away from the domination of their
parents. They were determined to show their parents and
"everybody" that they could break the ties that held them so
tightly to family discipline. Not until it was too late did these youth
realize they were taking with them all they possessed.

We are pilgrims and pioneers in life, and in every thought,
word, and deed we witness to the best and least of our hopes,
dreams, and purposes. When we face the times when the moral

ties are broken, it should be remembered we are giving a witness in our actions and reactions, and we are under heavy obligation to help others develop the kind of witness for God they want most to present. Running away to the far countries of place and condition may not be the best answer to life. Yet when we have run away, there remains the task of returning. The coming back may be to all we thought we had left. It may mean only a partial return to provide the opportunity for the development of new ideals and goals.

To all those who run away—and we all do in one fashion or another—there is no hope to be offered if we sit in judgment. Now we must change the burdens we bear. This begins at that very moment we see the pigsty in which we live. The recognition does not alter the pigsty, but is does make possible our leaving it for something better.

Let us not fear the far countries, but despise the running away. Let us remember that freedom never comes by the torturous route of escape. In the broad mercies of God shall we discover the only object toward which we can run and "not grow weary."

PRAYER:

Lord, how I want to run away. I detest this place in which I live, the seeming injustice of too much love or hate that sears all I touch. How I long to be a person, free to do and say all I think and will. Lord, hold thou my hand. Still the fever of my mind and heart. Keep patient the feet that would flee and the hands that would hold things of which I dream. For one brief, saving moment, let the clear breath of thy spirit move through me. Show me, O God, the burdens of life that are fastened in me. Teach me how to be free of them, and if I cannot be free, then teach me how to live with them. Above all, uphold me that I may stand in thy presence knowing it is not without honor simply to stand. Perhaps one day when I have gained the balance in my life, you will lead me gently to higher goals and nobler purposes, through Jesus our Savior. Amen.

Guilt and Shame

Read: *Hebrews 12:1-2*

> *" . . . who for the joy that was set*
> *before him endured the cross,*
> *despising the shame . . . ."*
> Hebrews 12:2b

Joy—cross—shame! These words leap out at us capturing the mind. For the joy that was to come, our Lord endured the guilt of the cross and the shame of the crucifixion. No joy is to be found in guilt and shame, but here is the making of joy. Difficult as it may seem, this is the logic of God's way. If we are not mistaken we can see it in the witness of those who form our "great cloud of witnesses."

Stephen, "full of grace and power," (Acts 6:8a) was guilty of being a follower of the Christ. The conviction carried with it the shame of stoning. Paul, guilty of being an apostle of our Lord, suffered the shame of beatings, imprisonments, and stonings. The evidence of these men was drawn out "for the joy that was set before them." But guilt and shame are not always so experienced. The seeming joys after which one stretches may produce both guilt and shame without any justifiable satisfactions.

Not infrequently, the moral ties are broken for no better reason than the satisfaction of adolescent curiosity or immature rebellion. It is not uncommon for adults to find themselves caught in the twilight of choices that have seemed necessary to escape difficulties that the mind will not face and that the spirit is incapable of comprehending. In any event, the twins of guilt and shame enslave us. The clear terror of our condition is not unlike that spoken in *The Vicar of Wakefield:*

> When lovely woman stoops to folly,
> And finds too late that men betray,
> What charm can soothe her melancholy?
> What art can wash her guilt away?[36]

And in the full consciousness of guilt comes its inevitable companion, as Rudyard Kipling described:

Till the fatted souls of the English were
scourged with the thing called Shame.[37]

In the grasp of so formidable an enemy, we are compelled to see
to what hope we can place our trembling hands.

The prophet Isaiah is recorded by Matthew to have said, "He
(Jesus) took our infirmities and bore our diseases" (Matthew
8:17b). Again we read, "He himself bore our sins in his body on
the tree" (1 Peter 2:24a). Our guilt is not our burden alone if we
can learn how to let God share it with us. Wayne E. Oates shares
this experience of a pastor and a young woman who had a
problem with guilt. "Her pastor encouraged her to continue her
search in prayer for a new meaning in life, a knowledge of the
love and presence of God, and a cleared-up mind about her
future.... He encouraged her to go home and lay the whole thing
down for a while, asking God how to pick it up again. This she
did with courage. In the 'act of surrender,' as Tiebout calls it, her
prayer was answered."[38]

In the deepest meaning of the word, guilt is something for
which payment must be made. A crime or trespass must be
expunged in some way. God has made forgiveness possible, but
the individual has to come to grips with the problem of guilt. This
is a very personal matter in which God, the minister, and the
counselor may give us great help. The final measure of success
depends upon our ability to witness to the joy of freedom from
guilt in God-forgiven and personal-righted relationships. For this
kind of joy the anguish through which tormenting guilt leads will
surely see the decrease of sorrow and the increase of happiness.

There is however, a larger context of guilt known as shame.
This is something that the individual trespasser shares, and in a
much deeper sense, the friends and family of the guilty person
share.

Life has its difficult moments and such was the case when
Sharon came to see her minister. The high school girl's father
and mother came with her. The moral ties that the family had
attempted to establish were broken and Sharon was expecting a
child. The parents did not seek to understand their daughter.
They could think of nothing but the terrible shame that was theirs.
True, all three were caught in shame and one in guilt. "But there
is hope," the minister pointed out. "Sharon is hungry for love.

85

Now you can show her the most vital kind of love in the world. In her guilt and shame stand side by side. She needs you and you will find new joys as a family when, in love, you support her. Others in society—her friends and the people of her community—may shun your daughter. Take her with you and accept her as a part of your family. Include her in all you do. The moral ties that are broken were strained to parting in the dirth of love and affection. Your daughter found her need for affection satisfied in another's life."

In the forefront of life, there must be joys for which we are willing to labor. When we set them before us we realize that they will cost us pain and sometimes guilt and shame. Like the Jesus-followers of the first century, let us set the joy of God before us and endure all things to achieve fellowship with this way of life. This does not mean that the ways of righteousness will not be tried, nor the moral ties broken, but it does mean there is a holy fellowship that forgives, reunites the parted fibers of love, and keeps us in that way which is not less than his kingdom.

PRAYER:

The bruised of the earth are thine, O Lord. I am bruised, for in my heart there is a burden of guilt. Like a millstone, it hangs in my soul and keeps my days out of balance. Neither sun, nor moon, nor stars seem in place and I have lost confidence in thee and in myself. Lord, help me to bear this uneven burden and come to the knowledge that thou wilt take my sins upon thyself. This forgiveness which is more than words is my need. My only hope is the power of thy strength which will lift me up and help me stand.

Beyond this sense of guilt stands the shame, which like a fog, has come upon me and those near me. O Lord, grant to me and to those with me the power of thy presence that we may stand in a fellowship unbroken. Let me despise all shame, knowing it is enough to have the guilt. And, by thy grace so lead my life that such guilt and shame as are mine may be counted true because I have dared to witness for thee. Thus would I have my life filled with thy joy for which all costs are insignificant wherein righteousness knits again the broken moral ties of life. Amen.

Out of the Depths

Read: Luke 18:9-14

"God, be merciful to me a sinner!"
Luke 18:13b

All of us are sinners. This fact cannot be washed out with the simple prayer, "God be merciful to me a sinner!" The evidence of a life turning from sin to righteousness is to be found in deeds bearing the mark of God's wisdom. Had the publican in the temple gone on to list his many crimes against neighbor and God, the moral fabric of life might well have been ruptured in the deepest of spiritual context. It is one thing to sin and know it, and quite another matter to sin and boast about it. The secret confessional is proper because it never publishes either unrighteousness or the sinner in public. While open testimonials may not be improper to spiritual integrity, they do possess a portion of danger in that the confessor is thereby provided the drama of public hearing. Jesus observed that those who prayed in public to be heard for their many words had their reward. The reward of witnessing of our many sins may be no greater than to be heard of by others.

While moral ties of life are strained, it is not man who will restore them, but God. When we fall to the depths of human degradation and the lamp of the soul has been crushed under the awful weight of self-righteousness, then our only hope rests in the power of the Eternal. It is God who can resurrect that which is lost and renew that which is tarnished. If we dare to speak of our long list of sins, it must only be with the spirit of complete humility that breathes from the anguish of a soul being restored by the mercy and forgiveness of God. Let it be sufficient for each of us to cry out, "God, be merciful to me a sinner!"

The publican is rejecting himself at worst. Equally, he is incapable of self-righteousness. The turning point from the deeps of life at its worst is that magnificent moment when we understand we can do little through our own powers. It is that thrilling discovery that "there is a Higher Power that has more faith in man than he has in himself." But, as an axle does not make a

87

wheel, so this turning point is not a victory. It is the beginning of new life. From this central determination we must move out to the new life. It is not enough to recognize that we are living in a pigsty. We must find our way out of the spiritual squalor into the refreshing avenues of renewed living.

Praying in the temple was the first real hope in the publican's sorrowful life. What happened outside the temple as a result of this discovery would prove the real test. Maslow and Mittlemann have provided us with a careful list of the rounds on the ladder that lead out of the depths to the joys of Christ-like living. Look at this list carefully to determine your areas of greatest need:

1. Adequate security feelings—good rapport with family, friends, co-workers. A sense of belonging!

2. Adequate and firmly based self-esteem—seeing ourselves for what we are; accepting our limitations and our abilities without jealousy or revolt.

3. Adequate free expression of the personality—cast aside our role in life and be what we are. Be unafraid or unashamed of anger, laughter, joy, and happiness.

4. Adequate self-knowledge—a willingness to come to grips with our motives, goals, desires. Fear of what we are paralyzes our understanding of ourselves.

5. Adequate and efficient contact with and use of reality—seek to know life and things as they are—not as we imagine them to be. Live today and "be not anxious for tomorrow."

6. Adequate emotionality—have no fear of one's emotions. Develop a sympathy for the emotions of others.

7. Adequate integration and consistency of personality—have ideals, goals, and purposes and stick to them. Do not shun conflict but let it lead to choice. Choose because you think, reason, pray.

8. Adequate life goals—establish realistic goals and be willing to give the effort and work in thought and deed to achieve these goals.

9. Ability to accept love, affection, and support—accept the love of family, friends, social group, and most particularly, the love of God. [39]

When you have thought and prayed on these matters, the turning point of life begins to take on the body of real purpose. With the soul open now to the will of God, we are ready to be led by the Divine Spirit into a completely new way of life. At the root of the whole matter is our unique ability to love God. This is what the publican realized and what he did when he prayed, "God be merciful to me a sinner!" St. Therese expressed it clearly in this way: "Until two days before her death she wished to be alone at night, however, notwithstanding her entreaties, the Infirmarian used to rise several times to visit her. On one occasion she found our little invalid with hands clasped and eyes raised to Heaven. 'But what are you doing?' she asked; 'you should try to sleep.' 'I cannot, dear Sister, I suffer too much! Then I pray....' 'And what do you say to Jesus?' 'I say nothing, I love Him!'"[40] Out of the depths of sin and distress our lives must come. And it will be so, not by what we do, but by our ability to "love him." Let us search our hearts, let us open our souls in prayer, and let the spirit of God be merciful to us and lead us.

PRAYER:

Forgive me, O Lord, for my many grievous sins. Much more I stand in need of being forgiven for wanting to look upon my sins. It is more than a verbal recounting of evil, it is a near love. I feel like a moth irresistibly drawn to a destructive fire. Lord, I need more than simple forgiveness. I am in need of thy spirit to possess me! Yes, Lord, "forgive me" but not that only. Have mercy on me. My wretchedness cannot be overcome by my feeble strength. There is no power in my words and my thoughts are blurred. Only thy presence can restore me. "Cast out sin and enter in." Let the flaming witness of thy spirit be in me. I want to love thee...I want to...I do love thee because thou hast placed the spirit of thy love within my soul. Thank you, God, for now I no longer recount my sins, but seek to name my opportunities to express my love—thy love—which holds me firm. Amen.

VII

In Faith
and When We
Are Desolate

From Gloom to Glory

Read: John 21:1-3;
Acts 1:6-11

" . . . and you shall be my witnesses in
Jerusalem and in all Judea and Samaria
and to the end of the earth."
Acts 1:8b

Despair is a quality of the spirit that descends like a wet, sticky blanket to smother the mind and still the soul. It defies definition but not knowledge. From the ragged scraps that the mind can describe, the soul fashions understanding too deep for words. Job expresses the matter vividly:

For my sighing comes as my bread,
and my groanings are poured out like water.
For the thing that I fear comes upon me,
and what I dread befalls me.
I am not at ease, nor am I quiet;
I have no rest; but trouble comes.
Job 3:24-26

This is a fair beginning at describing the pit of black despair that comes to all who feel absolutely alone, bereft of both God and others. It is out of this gloom that we can strike ourselves down. In such melancholy, the hopeless does the meaningless thing and seeks to still the throb of life that, though changed, cannot be silenced.

In some small way, Peter reflects this kind of utter despondency when, after the crucifixion of our Lord, he gathers his friends about him declaring, "I am going fishing." In more detailed fashion, Peter was giving vent to frustration stemming from his denial of the Master. The "Big Fisherman" was making active the latent disappointment in Christ who had refused to be an earthly king. The kingdom had gone a-glimmering, the cross

93

was the victor, and the temple rulers had carried the day and the cause. It was high time, according to Peter, to return to the more sensible task of his early trade of fishing.

Lest we think too harshly of Peter, let us admit we have each felt the same kind of bitter gloom. Once faith of a lovely marriage blossomed in life only to be dashed by circumstances that have long since been lost in the crosscurrents of conflict. Once in faith we rode forth as young, modern Galahads seeking the Holy Grail of peace. Once we dared to challenge the timidity of another and and steel ourselves to hurt. Now in disillusionment of human motives and in the vise of suffering, faith seems a feeble weapon. Could it be that we have been unable to use our faith at the point it most needs to be used, to believe that faith is itself useful.

Reading from the apostles' side of time, we can understand their problems of despair. But we have two thousand years of history, and that gives us considerable advantage in terms of perspective. The apostles had no such privilege save as faith made it possible for them to see the unseen. Surely, it must have seemed grandiose when Jesus said to this gloomy group, "and you shall be my witnesses in Jerusalem and in all Judea and Samaria and to the end of the earth." Yet tradition has it that Paul and Peter went to Rome, Thomas to India, and others to the ends of the earth.

Nothing can destroy the blackness of despair restoring the glory of God intended so adequately as faith. It must be faith in the very act of faith itself. It must be faith that delivers us a perspective of the Divine. The poet Swinburne gives the matter to us pointedly:

> Faith in faith established evermore
> Stands a sea-mark in the tides of time.[41]

Faith is not some tool we use half expecting it to break at the first strong encounter. The one who dares to use this gift of God as a tranquilizer to escape some immediate trial has no faith at all. There are times when we can have no reasonable belief in God or in each other. The *how* of life cannot be fathomed. The *why* of life is limp in the mind. The place and time of circumstance is not predictable. Our forebears once believed the earth was flat, encased by four corners over the edge of which a person could fall to destruction. By faith, in still deeper wisdom and broader knowledge, the old understanding has been forsaken. Such a discovery belonged to those who dared to believe in a new faith. Slavery once seemed so entrenched in American life that it appeared hopeless for anyone to dream of any day when the public market of human flesh would pass. The new day of freedom and human dignity belonged to those who dared to believe against all hope. Dwight L. Moody was not blessed with many years of formal education, and his poor grammar would have been a deterrent to a lesser man. His faith that God would use him if he dared to believe in the Eternal was what led this humble man to a noble witness. In the midst of human gloom, glory begins to tremble, real, but unborn for those who believe in faith.

The first faint glimmer of glory begins to mushroom into reality when we discover our sense of perspective. The ability to concentrate upon any goal is difficult. The longer we are asked to keep our powers of attention operative, the greater the burden. The disciples who followed Jesus were constantly asking for a sign. They sought to penetrate the future. To this vexing problem Jesus replied, as Luke records, "It is not for you to know times or seasons which the Father has fixed by his own authority" (Acts 1:7). The Master would reveal to us an understanding of the present. Faith takes the question marks of the future and clothes them in the assurance of God's matchless grace. The firmest kind of faith springs from a perspective about the present. Read the gospel stories again. Erase from your mind all you remember about them. Let the words lead you as the action led those of that first century. In such an attitude Stephen's sermon is a blaze of glory. Paul's missionary journeys are a grand adventure in faith. Jesus' teachings become a day-by-day thrill of new light evaporating the shadows of daily problems. Seeping into the mind of the reader comes the unseen, yet present, spirit of faith by which those people lived. Stephen dared to speak by faith even if it meant death; Paul continued to teach even when rejected; Jesus constantly met people's needs even when righteousness was beaten down by pride. The Christian witness is not immune to gloom. His glory is that he has the only element that can change gloom to glory. It is by faith that we live in the perspective of the immediate, leaving tomorrow and the future to the gracious keeping of God. It is only under such circumstances that we can manage the pilgrim-pioneer task of living to bear our witness to the end of the earth.

PRAYER:

Lead me gently, O Lord, for my faith is often more fragile than the tempered steel of daily need. Again and again my soul is cast down and no light of hope steals into my gray days. In the chasm of such despair, the pressure of human events and the smallness of my faith seem too weak to keep me from being crushed. It is for faith in faith itself that I plead, O God. The inner spirit to dare to believe in thee, that is what I need. Lead me, Father, to understand the faith of those who have gone before me. Help me to identify myself with them. Though I dare not reach out and possess thy grace, Lord, reach out to me and possess my life. Let the power of thy grace enfold the tenderness of my unbelief. Restore in me the "leaning spirit" which rejects even the weakness of my own strength. In the keeping of thy mercy lead me from gloom to glory. This I pray in assurance that you will possess me and let my life be a witness to thy glory. Amen.

Clothes of Desolation

Read: Acts 7:54—8:1

> " . . . and the witnesses laid down their
> garments at the feet of a young
> man named Saul."
> Acts 7:58b

The cold black strokes of a charcoal drawing could not more clearly depict the powerful force of action than these brief words concerning the "witnesses" at the stoning of Stephen. These men were gathered to bear testimony to the death of the one who, by their deed, became the first Christian martyr. By ancient law, the "witnesses" were designated to cast the first stones.

Precise evidence of the vigor of their deed is not left in doubt when we read they "laid down their garments." No catching movement of the clothing must destroy the accuracy of their missiles. In a very real sense, every witness needs this same bold approach to the tasks that rest upon him.

The men and women who race in the Olympic games know they must be free from the encumbrance of extra clothing. Nothing must catch at the body to slow it down. The athlete understands the need for the muscles to be used for the race only and not to struggle against snagging garments. The writer of Hebrews spells this out for us: "Let us also lay aside every weight, and sin which clings so closely, and let us run with perseverance the race that is set before us" (Hebrews 12:1a). In a slightly different sense, but with equal recognition of the need to be free of entangling baggage, our Lord instructed the disciples, "Take no gold, nor silver, nor copper in your belts, no bag for your journey, nor two tunics, nor sandals, nor a staff" (Matthew 10:9-10a). The matter is obvious: The witness must be free of any entangling garment in order to do the task assigned.

Just as the body must be free to move decisively, so the soul must be free to seek God unencumbered. The clothes of desolation can encase the soul in such isolation as to still all apparent life. In the language of modern attire, we might suggest it is time for us to lay aside the suit of respectability, the belt of tolerance, and the shoes of pride. At least these garments that strangle the witness of the spirit must go.

The clothes of respectability have all but drained away any hope of spiritual life. The avid race for position has found us enslaved to subtle monsters that suck away the life-blood of the soul. Gray flannel suits become the trademark of Madison Avenue, where people have placed a dollar sign so deeply upon their values that the branding iron of profit has erased the virtue of moral integrity. The classy lines of a new automobile have cut so deep into our race for recognition that what we drive has come to speak louder of our character than what we are. Nurses dress in white, ministers in black, the would-be-successful businessman must never be without his coat. Encased in all these garments of modern respectability we have become slaves trying to speak of our importance through what meets the eye. Could it be that this very deadening race of respectability is the firmest sign of our real boredom and frustration with life? Could it be that these are the garments of our spiritual desolation?

Look again at this modern man. The bulging waistline of his physical craving is hindered by the belt of tolerance. If he is to be respectable, he must be banqueted, feted, and saturated. All this he must tolerate because he is bound by the steel band of conformity. The very instruments that are designed to give him hope to see powers beyond himself are now the straps that confine him in the straightjacket of being and accepting the very conduct that is secretly abhorred. So long has this process been going on that he has lost much of his moral integrity. Could it be that this is one of the garments that must be torn away? Could it be that such tolerance has led us to believe in so little that life has lost its meaning?

Take another look. The shoes that have been carefully manicured each night reflect nothing more important than one's own image upside down. They tell the world of the consummate pride with which we walk. Better not risk walking in the dirty places of life. We might spoil the shine. Step lightly in the compromising situations lest someone see us and we would be asked to bear witness of where we are. Walk boldly here because we are in safe company where nothing is at risk. Could it be that our very shoes of pride are a symbol of false respectability?

Ask yourself these questions. Then think of the garments flung aside by the witnesses who refused to be trammeled. Think of Francis of Assisi who walked bare-footed over the snow, rocks, and sand to preach the love of Christ. Think of the Bishop of Canterbury who refused to tolerate the encroachments of Henry VIII, even when such an intolerant stand could and did cost him his life. Think of Albert Schweitzer who cast away the comfort and honor of teaching, or the dignity of a master of music, that he might walk, teach, and heal among the unclothed natives of Africa.

The Christian witness is called to action. Nothing must impede our movement as we labor under the orders of the Lord. With the same bold strokes of those who cast the first Christian martyr into existence, let us lay down the garments of our desolation. Free from these spiritual nets that can only lead to soul destruction, let us rise to bear the testimony of God that lives, by God's grace, within us.

PRAYER:

O Lord, thou knowest the secret garments of my soul which weigh me down. The lusts, the greed, the pride, the false tolerance—they all rush up and down in my being. These evil spirits whose name is "legion" pull and tear at my very life. In the fevered pitch of their wild escapades, Lord, enter into my life and cleanse my soul. Only when thy presence is in me can there be any hope amid all my desolation. When, O God, thou art with me, then shall these robes of restriction slip away. Forgive me for seeking to stand in the pretense of my finery before the glory of thy face. Let me dare to stand naked of soul before thee knowing that thou wilt clothe me in a right mind, a gentle spirit, and a redeeming love. Unto these new garments let me move with haste that my life may spell out the witness of thy will through Jesus Christ, my Lord. Amen.

Out of Denial

Read: Acts 22:3-21

> *"I am Jesus of Nazareth whom you
> are persecuting."*
> Acts 22:8b

Three amazing things happened to Saul. He denied his own best intentions, rejected the will of God, and discovered God breaking through human denial to the end that Saul the persecutor became Paul the evangelist. What took place in Saul's life is precisely that which forms itself in each life. God confronts us in the darkness of our denial that we, sensing some small part of divine light, may move into the clearer paths of righteousness. This is the struggle in each pilgrim-pioneer life that leads to the fulfillment of witness for God.

Denial is self-contained in that, as Paul said, it is "fears within." We reject the will of God either because we do not accept the purposes and conditions of that will, or because we fear the qualities of life that such acceptance would make necessary. In Saul's case it was impossible to accept God's will because of previous training and because of firm commitments to Judaism. Deep within this powerful man was a fear of what the thrust of Christ's teachings would do to his loyalty to the faith of his ancestors. In the matrix of stout loyalty on the one hand and mingled fears on the other, denial emerged in the form of powerful persecution to the Christians. In this condition, Saul was denying his own best ability to sense the will of God and to use his own superior abilities of human thought. Personal denial became rejection of God.

Into this framework moved the spirit of the Divine. Saul was confronted on the way to Damascus by the presence of Christ. What had begun as "fightings without and fears within" was now a personal divine-human encounter in the form of Christ and Saul. The situation became clear in the statement of our Lord, "I am Jesus of Nazareth whom you are persecuting." In this climactic moment, the cloud of doubt, fear, and uncertainty had been penetrated. Saul had come face to face with the truth. This was his most perilous moment. Would he remain Saul of confusion and inner turmoil or would he become Paul who was "more than confident" through Jesus Christ? We know the end of the matter because Saul became Paul on the Damascus Road. But do we know the end of the divine confrontation for our own lives?

In each of us lives the Saul and Paul of our nature seeking for dominance. Is faith to be extinguished by our "fightings and fears"? Will the purposes of God rise above the doubts that lurk in our minds? Is it possible for us to meet Christ and walk with him or will we turn aside to what seems at the moment a more convenient way?

When all the forces of human doubt have crowded out the sparkle of hope, we "beat the air vainly." It is in such moments that God confronts us with some climactic choice. This moment came to Francis of Assisi when, as a young man, he was confronted with the misshapen forms and disease-ridden bodies of the lepers. More often than not, the choice is made more quietly and less dramatically. Luke tells us of a rich man who did not see the choice placed in his life in the form of a "poor man named Lazarus" (Luke 16:19ff). Beggars were a common sight and we, like the rich man, would hardly see a climactic choice in the form of such a person.

Faith takes over and is reborn in us at that precise moment we see each "fighting without and fear within" as the privilege of choosing for the will of God. Every one of these in need stands before us as Christ before Saul saying, "I am Jesus of Nazareth whom you are persecuting." Victory over our doubts and fears comes only to those who move from denial to acceptance of Christ.

PRAYER:

Enter, O Lord, into our lives. Penetrate the darkness of our doubts and fears. Lay bare our lives encrusted by the pressures of discontent from the world and relieve us from the inner fears of uncertainty. Confront us with the clear truth of thy holy presence. Let the light of thy truth cleanse our vision and the power of thy spirit purify our minds and hearts. Let faith spring up renewed in our hearts that we may be servants whose lives and deeds are acceptable in thy sight. As thou art quick to forgive our feeble ways, let us be alert to accept thy paths of righteousness. In darkness we deny thee. Give us, O God, thy light that we may affirm our loyalty to thee. Though tremblingly we enter into thy presence, may our lives be renewed that our every word and deed may bespeak the affirmation of our trust in thee. Amen.

Prayer Unceasing

Read: Romans 1:8-15

*"For God is my witness . . . that without ceasing
I mention you always in my prayers . . . ."*
Romans 1:9

Prayer is more than a personal matter. It is a fellowship. Paul, in writing to the Christians at Rome, makes it clear that the purpose of his prayers is "that I may impart to you some spiritual gift to strengthen you, that is, that we may be mutually encouraged by each other's faith, both yours and mine" (Romans 1:11-12). Full evidence of Paul's awareness of the fellowship of prayer is seen in the last chapter of the Roman letter. Here Paul named thirty-one different individuals, and a host of others are included. This fellowship of faith sustained by prayer "without ceasing" is drawn in the sharp lines of personal lives. The interwoven nature of this spiritual fellowship sets forth the tapestry of active faith.

Compare this faith that is fellowship and upheld by prayer unceasing with the shallow faith that we so often call a "personal faith." It is possible that George Eliot reflects this lighter vein when she writes:

So faith is strong
Only when we are strong, shrinks when we shrink.[42]

Such a thought leads us to believe that faith is based upon what one does. In reality, faith is God's gift to us and we are strong when it leads us to increased spiritual power. Indeed, it is not our strength but strength expended that matters. Richard Burton shows us the real secret when he leads our thoughts:

Not in the morning vigor, Lord, am I
Most sure of Thee, but when the day goes by
To evening and, all spent with work, my head
Is bowed, my limbs are laid upon my bed.
Lo! in my weariness is faith at length,
Even as children's weakness is their strength.[43]

There remains the question, then, of how we shall pour out our strength to the end that faith, undergirded by prayer, may uplead us from doubt and fear. Paul gives us crystal insight into this matter when he observes, "For God is my witness…that without ceasing I mention you always in my prayers" (Romans 1:9). Through prayer, life becomes a fellowship of faith.

Prayer points up our faith and fellowship with God who is able to do for us what we cannot do for ourselves. Jesus knew the power of prayer to renew faith. He discovered it on the Mount of Temptation and among the hills of Galilee, and on the rocky ground of Gethsemane, which nestled in the shadows of the wall of Jerusalem. When human energy had been sapped, our Lord was renewed through prayer unceasing. Robert Louis Stevenson soon learned that physical strength is not enough. Perhaps this is the reason so much of what he wrote shows the upward thrust of his great faith. No small part of what Stevenson wrote is cast in the spirit of prayer. In St. Giles Church in Edinburgh and inscribed on Stevenson's memorial may be found these words,

Give us grace and strength to forbear and to persevere. Give us courage and gaiety and the quiet mind. Spare to us our friends, soften to us our enemies. If it may not, give us the strength to encounter that which is to come, that we may be brave in peril, constant in tribulation, temperate in wrath, and in all change of fortune, and down to the gates of death, loyal and loving to one another.

Faith is that fellowship that emerges from our prayers unceasing to guide our feet in the paths of light.

Also, prayer illuminates our faith and our human fellowship. Paul gives evidence of this in the first chapter of Romans and again in 1 Corinthians. This is no human strength but the establishment of a holy community of concern. Paul, in Asia Minor, is concerned with the Christians at Corinth; in Corinth with the Christians at Rome; at Ephesus he prays with the elders of the church as they meet on the seashore. In all his travels he is concerned with the "necessity of the saints" in Jerusalem. The light of prayer reaches out in increasing radiance to bind the early church together. Prayer binds heart to heart and manifests all in one fellowship before the presence of God. Prayer banishes hatred, suspicion, doubt, and fear of others because as we commend others to God, we become identified with them and with our Lord.

When faith is only personal it strikes but a single tone that has neither harmony nor overtone. When faith becomes fellowship through prayer, we compose a symphony that moves all musicians and hearers, and none are free of the haunting memory of its beauty.

PRAYER:

Lord, deliver me from being a spiritual monotone when you have made it possible through prayer for me to produce the symphonies of the soul. Forgive me for believing that thy concern is for me only. Let thy spirit witness to concern for me which unclogs the spiritual springs of my soul. Let the clear, clean message of thy will pour through me to others. Teach me, O God, that in the power of such faith thy kingdom grows, thy power enfolds each of us, and thy will is done perfectly upon earth as it is in heaven. Let me pray without ceasing. When my voice and lips can no longer speak, let my mind carry the message of the fellowship of faith. Thus, would I hold thy light in my heart and illumine the ways of thy children that all may walk with thee, through the leadership of thy Son, Jesus Christ. Amen.

Victory of Confession

Read: 1 Timothy 6:11-16

*". . . when you made the good confession in
the presence of many witnesses."*
1 Timothy 6:12b

Paul, enumerating the aims of Christian life, observes that faith is essential to the devotee of Christ. There is no doubt that Paul is aware of the origins of faith in the human heart. He is equally conscious of the importance of the witnesses to confession. Both the individual in confession and the witness are bound together as part of one's living faith.

At the outset of the Christian life, the individual makes a "confession of faith." Generally this is a high moment of new dedication where the confessor is surrounded by a large number of interested members of family and friends. High emotions are countered by deep spiritual awareness. All of us can remember, "when you made the good confession in the presence of many witnesses."

In converse condition Paul reminds Timothy that it will not always be so easy to confess Christ. There will be times when we, like our Lord, will have to stand alone before unfriendly witnesses. "Jesus who in his testimony before Pontius Pilate made the good confession." Our Lord was alone and the witnesses were hostile.

We conclude the Christian is under obligation to confess Christ "in season and out of season." But there is a deeper meaning to this clear contrast of conditions that bore in upon the Christian witness. There is a sense in which such extremes of condition merge to suggest we are under obligation to confess Christ constantly. It is in this larger context of continual expression that we come to grips with the real victory of confession.

Upon this level of confession, the very things that have cloyed our faith become the opportunities that portray the power of our deeds. William M. Hunter, telling of a personal victory in the life of his daughter, leads our thoughts with these words: "Generally speaking, whenever a person has faith, he tends not only to pray in the more formal, or spoken sense of the word, but to live on the assumption that one's needs are also one's prayer."[44] In writing to the Christians at Corinth, Paul expressed the same thought when he said, "For a wide door for effective work has opened to me, and there are many adversaries" (1 Corinthians 16:9). When we seek to confess, our problems become privileges to bear witness to our faith.

A.W. Fortune, noted teacher, author, and preacher, found the problem of sudden blindness as an opportunity to witness to his confession of faith. "I resolved," wrote Dr. Fortune, "that I would make the best of the situation.... I would not become rebellious, or permit myself to blame God for the affliction which had come to me." The highway of such Christian witness reached a high level as he continued, "In fact, I can see no reason why this should not have happened to me as well as to anyone else."[45] In the true spirit of a pilgrim-pioneer follower of our Lord, A.W. Fortune continued to read by Braille, to write, lecture, and preach. He discovered he could witness for his Lord in every circumstance of life. This is victory in a life of continued confession.

It is imperative that we learn how to confess Christ in the normal experiences of life. Sometimes we can rise to high challenges when the ordinary dulls our perception. Think of what it means to pray day after day or teach a class in church school Sunday after Sunday, or to remember to call regularly on those in distress. These tasks seem to lack color. Recently an elder, who had taken communion to an elderly woman not able to attend services for many months, was complaining about this seemingly routine task. When told the woman had died a few days after receiving communion, the seemingly ordinary event took on new meaning. We are called to let the leaven of faith work in our lives to the end we confess Christ in the level events of our lives as in the times of great challenge.

This is what we might call the confessional life. That way of human conduct that never misses an opportunity to speak the faith we hold in terms of human conduct. Whether surrounded by friendly witnesses or foes of our faith, we find the real victories of God when we give our testimony to all in every condition. Faith may be challenged by the desolation of human hurt, but deep within the body of faith is its own life, which is not different than the image of our Lord seeking to capture and recapture our lives to bear testimony to him.

PRAYER:

Lord, thou hast led me through the vales of despair when it seemed my soul was dissipated into nothingness and my thoughts were vapor. Thou hast gently forgiven me when I refused to grapple with the burdens of grief, sorrow, disappointment, and fear. Thou hast restored my soul when, worn by the constant pressure of life, I found neither the hope nor the energy to bestir myself from the couch of self-pity. Thou art, indeed, my light and my hope. A new life has been fused into the dying embers of my soul. Where once I was desolate, now I am full of hope; where once I was melancholy, now I have new purposes; where once my thoughts were at best concerned with myself, now I can focus my life upon thee. My soul rejoices with the new hope thou hast given to me. Lord, let thy "everlasting arms" uphold me and thy gentle spirit lead me that my days shall become jewels of confession in word and deed amid the diadem of thy glory. Amen.

VIII

In Work and When the Lamp Flickers

Character

Read: Matthew 15:10-20

*"For out of the heart come evil thoughts,
murder, adultery, fornication, theft,
false witness, slander."*
Matthew 15:19

"How a person gets his money indicates his character." The reverse is equally true. "A person's character determines how he gets his money." Character and work are interwoven. At the best of life, it is one's character that determines the quality of deed. And it is this very fact that, though patently simple, is so frequently overlooked. The Christ illuminated this matter with clear language when he declared, "For out of the heart come evil thoughts, murder, adultery, fornication, theft, false witness, slander." Character is the result of inner and spiritual development. Work is the external extension of one's character.

Before we take up any task we must make certain choices. Are we fitted for this work? Are we physically able to render an acceptable service? Will we find adequate living conditions in this employment? Can we have sufficient income to maintain a proper kind of life? Finally, and this is the question we seldom ask, will our life find its fullest meaning in this position? The first four questions deal with material concerns. The last question is a matter of the spirit that will be answered by the dimensions of character.

If we are Christian witnesses in everything we do then the last question strikes at the heart of what we do with life. It is not a matter of choice but a matter of compunction. As servants of Christ we are always confronted with the question of whether or not our daily work provides opportunity for us to declare our faith in our Master. Not a few earnest followers of the Galilean have discovered their labor challenged by the ethical and moral implications of the gospel. Albert A. Schulke was one of the scientists who helped make plutonium at Washington University, St. Louis, Missouri. Interested in the work at hand, the larger implication of ethical concern had not been confronted. After the first nuclear bomb was dropped in World War II, the utter helplessness and confusion of the heart was reflected in these words: "All we could do was wait. When we did hear of the devastation wrought by the bomb, we just sat in the laboratory, speechless. There wasn't anything to say then."[46] The tasks to which we lay our hands will sooner or later be challenged by the stature of our character.

This inner spiritual quality may sometimes be called integrity. Character has the quality of integrity that comes from the inner person. From such inner vitality and integrity emerges that life which must always ask of every work to which it is called, "Will my life find its fullest meaning in this position?"

In final analysis, this is the spiritual confrontation in the realm of labor that raises man to the noble class of servant or reduces him to the mean condition of servitude. When life finds its fullest meaning, that life is being poured out in service. In this context, each one of us becomes a witness to Christ in the pilgrim-pioneer experiences of life.

A clothier in Southwest America declared, "We sell only the best quality merchandise. To sell less would be to defraud our customers." This was more than a business slogan, it was the extension of inner character and integrity into the dimensions of work.

You are surrounded by a host of earnest workers, business-men, businesswomen, and professional people who toil out their days to fulfill the highest qualities of character. If, as Jesus said, such negative characteristics as evil thoughts, theft, false witness, and slander can emerge from the heart, then it is possible for the higher attributes of good thoughts, honest truth telling, and Christian witness to spring from the heart. All those who see their work as a sacrament of life are living what Samuel Smiles wrote in the nineteenth century,

> Sow a Thought, and you reap an Act;
> Sow an Act, and you reap a Habit;
> Sow a Habit, and you reap a Character;
> Sow a Character, and you reap a Destiny.[47]

The task of the Christian is to let the light of inner character and integrity so fill the dimension of our deeds that we are capable of reaping a "destiny" that is no less than to share God's kingdom.

PRAYER:

Lord, let me give my heart to my work. Let the truth of thy spirit envelop my life to produce a character of righteousness. Let me learn how to express thy righteousness through the sinews of my labor. Forgive me, Lord, when the soot of human self besmirches my soul and profit becomes larger than service. Rid my soul of every selfish motive which beckons me to comfort and ease. Enlarge in my life every divine-like thought and deed which ennobles my character to speak thy words and to work for thy truth. Let the constancy of thy truth become the line of my integrity. Prepare in me the destiny of thy kingdom wrought by thy service to us, and which, in turn we humbly share with others. O Lord, make of me a worthy workman for thine own glory and the good of my fellow man, which is not less than to make my life find its fullest meaning, with the help of our Master, who was a Master workman. Amen.

Objectives

Read: James 5:1-6

"Your gold and silver have rusted, and their rust will be evidence against you and will eat your flesh like fire."
James 5:3

"How a person spends his money indicates his values." Money, which is the product of our work, is the convenient element of barter. Character, on the other hand, determines the kind of work to which we give ourselves. On the other hand our toil is an expenditure, and the things for which we spend ourselves reveal our sense of values.

Look at the work you are doing and ask yourself these questions: Am I working for money? Am I working for prestige? Do I expend myself in my job in order to find acceptance in my society? Why am I investing myself in my work? All of us need to ask ourselves these questions again and again. These are the questions that are close to our basic happiness and well-being. When we come to grips with these questions, we may discover the need to change jobs or professions. Our real unhappiness comes from not facing these questions and thereby burying our best ideals in the boredom of sameness. Even when we discover we must change our work, we may refuse only to find the inner tensions from such a refusal depriving us of both happiness and effectiveness.

What are the values or objectives in your work? Is it to make money? And if it is, what will your money buy? An interesting story emerged from the problems of a "sound-effects" specialist in the movie industry. Walt Disney was filming the story of King Midas. His technicians found they had to simulate the clinking of coins, for the shaking of real coins didn't create the correct sound. After a good deal of experimenting, someone discovered the technique that gave just the desired results—coiling and un-coiling a piece of chain. The subtle fact is no different today than in the time of James when he said, "Your gold and silver have rusted, and their rust will be evidence against you." When we witness to the making of money, it is a close coiling chain that is evidence against us.

And what will our money buy? A judge in Florida must have pondered on this when gangsters were taking him and his wife to their death. The judge offered them a $200,000 fortune for their freedom, but it did not deter the evil purpose of the killers. In the final analysis money cannot buy life, no more than it can purchase health or happiness.

By contrast, listen to what Henry Pope Mobley has to say as he wrote under the title of "Who Is Worthy?" in the July 15, 1959 issue of *Christian Observer*. "There is an island in the Caribbean Sea where a number of professors of Harvard and Yale spend their summer vacations. In a little church on that island, the adult Bible class is taught by a simple, poorly educated blacksmith. But

I have been told that the man has provided spiritual enrichment for those scholars who sit at his feet, and for years they have attended his Sunday school class. This blacksmith has dedicated the best he has to God and that is enough." The real secret to worthy values and good objectives rests upon the dedication of the best we have to God. The real test of our objectives comes when we determine the things we will purchase with our labor when the light of God makes clear to the divine sight what we have bought.

Melon invested a fortune to build a mission hospital in Haiti. Chopin spent his genius and health to give the world great music and his native Poland freedom. Francis of Assisi renounced the wealth of his merchant father to preach the redeeming love of God. A young man in Iowa dedicated himself to the Christian ministry despite the fact he was an only child and his parents had valuable holdings. The same thread of character and values runs through all these people.

We are each witnesses to God and the things our labor buys stand a mute but eloquent evidence of our work. What objectives do you have and on what values have you lifted the structure of your life? What evidence of your faith will endure as a testimony to your faith?

PRAYER:

Father of humankind, lead us gently in the alleys of our labor that we might walk in the avenues of thy service. Reveal to us the course of thy very truth which is ever-present. The flowers bear their bright blossoms to the eye's delight and the glory of thy handiwork. The trees send forth leaves to prove thy achievements and to shade the weary worker when he is tired. Teach us how to be as productive for thy good as are the flowers and the trees. Let the strength of my body, the alertness of my mind, the fires of my soul be molded into one living testimony of faith in thee. May my life be invested in thy service so that in the office, the classroom, or the marketplace, no one shall ever doubt that thou art my God. May my life purchase deeds of golden goodness with the service of unalloyed righteousness and as a lasting evidence of my subjection to thy sovereign will. In and through my daily work let me humbly serve thee now and all my days. Amen.

Adjustments

Read: Acts 16:6-10

". . . immediately we sought to go on into
Macedonia . . . . "
Acts 16:10b

Paul wanted to go into the northern part of Asia Minor to preach. The opportunity was denied and in its stead the missionary was led to Macedonia. This was a time of great change of direction. What seemed to be a simple choice actually moved the force of the Christian message westward to Rome from which it spread to Europe and the West. The response of Paul is not without importance. As soon as the challenge had been presented we are told, "Immediately we sought to go to Macedonia." When change presents itself, the opportunity must be grasped with all haste.

Changes confront us in our work. It may be a call to learn how to operate a new machine, travel a different trade route, or work in a new community. With one-third of America's population moving each year, this is the kind of situation that many face. Such changes call for adjustments, not a few of which must be made rapidly. We are called upon to change homes, friends, schools, churches. Sometimes it means learning new abilities or renewing abilities long forgotten. The adjustments are real and should be complete. Paul's vigor in accepting his challenge provides us with an insight into the spirit that may be of best help to us. When we move from one position or place to another, it becomes imperative that we accept the new opportunities and establish our full living. That is, we are under personal obligation to accept the new school, the new friends, the new home, and the new church with complete identity in our lives.

In a deeper sense there is a responsibility to see the changing fabric of life built upon the loom of changeless certainty. Wherever we go and whatever we do, we are still people and we are, in the Christian sense, children of God chosen to live in the pilgrim-pioneer way of life. No change need ask us for adjustments so severe as to destroy the stability of God's pattern. To

114

put it another way, we are to be Christian in every area of alteration that presents itself.

At this point, it is good to know that the apostles of our Lord were men who demonstrated their ability to be Christian in the work that they did. Peter, Andrew, James, and John continued their fishing enterprise and let the light of Christian faith show through their work. Paul supplied many of his needs with the labor of his own hands. He wrote to the Christians in Corinth saying, "And when I was with you and was in want, I did not burden any one.... I refrained and will refrain from burdening you in any way" (2 Corinthians 11:9). Frequently Paul supplied his own needs by working at his trade of tent-making. Even in his daily work he radiated his Christian faith.

A growing number of Christian men and women are realizing that their daily work is not divorced from their faith. In New York City a group of businessmen meet regularly for prayer before beginning their day's labor. In the lead mines of Missouri, a group of miners find time to pray deep in the shafts of the mines. A radio and television repairman in California has said, "As I work in a home repairing a television set I find the opportunity to speak for Christ." A juvenile officer in Mid-America believes he is making a Christian witness by helping young boys and girls find a better way of life. A businessman in Minnesota declares, "I am glad when I sell good merchandise because I believe it is a Christian deed." This is the climax to which we are called in Christian faith, that we may each make our witness for Christ amid the adjustments as well as the routine of our labor.

Beyond these experiences, another factor of human adjustment must be faced. There comes a time when the body is disabled or when the calendar marks off sufficient time that retirement becomes necessary. Of all the changes that life can afford, these can be some of the most severe.

Paul suffered a physical limitation that he referred to as "this thorn in the flesh." Viscount Horatio Nelson fought the battle of Trefalgar with the limitation occasioned by the loss of an arm and an eye in earlier life. Franklin D. Roosevelt carried the burdens of the American presidency with a body disabled by polio. Wherever we look, we find those who have made or are making adjustments to physical limitations. As a matter of fact, few if any are free from some form of such adjustment. The use of eyeglasses marks a physical limitation. From the small to the large needs, persons have moved to make life effective under every circumstance. Those most severely limited have been guided to new usefulness through rehabilitation efforts. The body may be limited, but life can be full of rich meaning. In every change we are called upon to bear testimony to our faith as we meet life and show it to be worthful.

Another of the great adjustments comes in the form of retirement. We will look at this more closely in the next section, but it must be noted here that this is another "Macedonian call" to a new and brighter work.

In every adjustment that we face, and there are many, we must come to see each change as a challenge to greater opportunity. And we must carry into each new task the constant evidence of our deep love for God and service for Christ. When our days and our labor are strong upon the thread of our love for God, no change is too difficult and each task is a candle lighted that all "may see your good works and give glory to your Father who is in heaven" (Matthew 5:16b).

PRAYER:

Let us pray in the spirit of William G. Tarrant when he wrote:

> My Master was a worker,
> With daily work to do,
> And he who would be like him
> Must be a worker too;
> Then welcome honest labor,
> And honest labor's fare,
> For where there is a worker,
> The Master's man is there.
>
> . . . .
>
> Then, brothers brave and manly
> Together let us be,
> For he, who is our Master,
> The Man of men was he;
> The men who would be like him
> Are wanted everywhere,
> And where they love each other
> The Master's men are there. [48]

116

Lord, in every adjustment of life let the work of my hands be the evidence of the meditations of my heart. May my life eagerly embrace each new opportunity to let thy glory show through the toil of my days. In the loving name of Jesus Christ, we pray. Amen.

New Meaning

Read: Matthew 13:47-52

> *". . . who brings out of his treasure what is*
> *new and what is old."*
> Matthew 13:52b

"Work," said Elton Trueblood, "is a window through which the divine light can shine in a peculiar way."[49] Dr. Trueblood introduced this statement with the words, "We (need to) hold before our minds the constant conviction that the common work we do is a share in the creation which is still unfinished...." There is a real sense in which one's work is always unfinished. Jesus, teaching in the parables of the kingdom, points out, "Therefore every scribe who has been trained for the kingdom of heaven is like a householder who brings out of his treasure what is new and what is old" (Matthew 13:52). This simple truth is given point when we look around the apartment or house in which we live. The total of all we see comprises a real part of our treasures. Some of these are old items that may have lost their utilitarian value but increase each year in their intrinsic value. Other items may be relatively new with many years of service ahead. The transient nature of all we behold speaks the onward course of life. As from our households we bring forth treasure that is new and is old, so from the days that comprise our years must flow a ceaseless tide of work that is both new and old.

The new is the richness of the immediate task that sees us fulfilling our appointed task in industry or office, in the marketplace or the classroom. The new product may be an appliance that makes easier the daily work of the home, or it may be an all-but-forgotten thought placed in a new life reaching out to maturity. This is the easily recognized accomplishment and it is new. But there is another dimension to our work. The very nature of work itself is a treasure that is very ancient. It is not unlike entering a second-hand book shop and finding an ancient copy of Socrates' *Phaedo*. On these ancient pages, the original and still new truth challenges the mind. In much the same way, the works that seem so new are really very old because they are part of work itself.

There is, therefore, the constant struggle to find new meaning in the old and the new of life. This is not easy when across the steady flow of work there is cast the stilling force of retirement. This is a new requirement of modern life. We can now be free of some of the drudgery that, in times past, enslaved till only death brought release. But this newfound freedom is not always welcome because not everyone has learned how to manage new meaning from old treasures.

Retirement lays heavy demands upon each of us. Frequently it is that moment when the light of the body's strength begins to falter. Work is still the economy by which we are at our greatest strength, but the work we have known for nearly a half-century must cease. Unless we give careful attention to new meanings for life, we may well see the flame of our witness cease to be a light for our feet or a lamp to the paths of others before the energy of life has ceased to exist.

New meaning in old treasures will tax our abilities when we face the requirements of retirement. There are four things we can do to prepare for this event that will overtake most of those who read these words. Long before retirement seems a reality, we can begin to prepare for that which seems remote. We are being called to a new profession that will require all our ability. The preparation will require us to learn new uses of time and talent. Hobbies are important but they are not the real heart of the matter. It will be necessary to learn how to adjust emotionally, mentally, and physically. Where once we had given our minds to great plans, we must now plan in a new order. We may develop skills and unpursued interests in creative new directions. We may work for the community or find our days filled with the work of the church. Whatever our work, it must still be that which requires our best efforts and provides us the joy of knowing our lives are still important.

The need to prepare emotionally may be distilled from a conversation between a minister and a husband and wife of his parish after the husband's retirement. The wife complained that her husband was under her feet all day. The husband complained that helping do the housework was not meaningful. This simple discussion highlights the fact that the divorce rate in America is rising among families where retirements are taking place. Emotionally, these families, who have been busy rearing a family and making a living, must now make a new adjustment to each other within the framework of the home. The recognition of this need in the years before retirement will greatly help to prepare for the actual event.

Beyond this preparation, and yet a part of it, is the understanding that though this kind of work changes in retirement, the labor must be important. Louis Pasteur was voted the greatest man in history by a group of students from several nations. The qualities that made him so important according to a psychologist were: "enthusiasm, courage, work, and ability to learn from his mistakes." To feel that life is important is the root through which life is made vital. A recent study instigated by one of America's large insurance companies indicates that a person will live better and longer when there is meaningful work to do. Some years ago a survey discovered that those who had no creative work after retirement had a life expectancy of two years or less. Those who found interesting labor could rightly expect to live several years beyond the otherwise limited expectancy. Even those who suffer limitation from heart trouble of any kind will live extra years if they can learn how to be creatively employed. It is not a matter of making a living. It is a matter of finding life worth living. An eighty-year-old man in Illinois lives on a limited income. In a state of reasonable health for his years, this man has learned how to make his days worthwhile. This man makes a practice of gathering up old toys that are broken and repairing them. Such work provides help to children and adults as well as making his days rich in creative work. This is another means of putting new meaning in old treasures.

Further, the person facing retirement can learn to develop a "yes" complex in life. The alternative to a "yes" complex about life leads us to the wisdom of Herbert Hoover, who, on his eighty-fifth birthday, said, "Those who retire without some occupation spend their time talking about their ills and their pills." Dr. and Mrs. George Breece learned how to find meaning in retirement. Both had taught for years and finished their regular responsibilities in America's great Northwest country. After a few years of teaching in a mission school in Kentucky—and that without pay—they went to Honolulu, Hawaii, to make their home. There they discovered a college that was staffed by retired teachers, and immediately engaged in teaching. Dr. Breece, in talking about this work observed, "I have never enjoyed teaching so much in all my life as I do now. My schedule is sufficient to keep me alert and interested, yet not so burdensome as to be a drudgery." The spirit of willingness to accept new challenges and enter into new experiences because we have a "yes" complex about life is another way of giving new meaning to the old treasure of work.

Finally, the approaching retirement provides the opportunity to grasp the values of aging. Knowledge comes quickly and is the treasure of youth. Wisdom is related to maturity and must be steeped in the mind and soul across the years. Retirement offers the positive value of wisdom that can be shared in a spirit of love with others. The way to give new meaning to old treasures is open to those whose years multiply their opportunities for Christian witness.

Prepare for the future and your work will never end. Through such preparation, your work will be a "window through which the divine light can shine in a peculiar way."

PRAYER:

Lord, guide me in these years of preparation for my finest witness to the faith which thou hast given me. Keep my mind from brittleness which allows not for growth in thought. Keep my soul from sluggishness which denies my acceptance of new challenges. Keep my life from satisfaction with all which I possess so I cannot know the new fields of service which are ever present. Enlarge the gratitude of my soul for the treasure of work which has compassed the years of my productivity. Let the nature of my soul, which lives in the house spent in labor, discern the high witness of love for thee. Thus, O God, would I find new meaning in the old treasure. In this discovery, Father, let the beauty of my testimony speak through the new tasks to which I consecrate my energy, my mind, my soul, and my days. Amen.

The Best Comes Last

Read: Acts 23:1-11

> *"Take courage, for as you have testified about me at Jerusalem, so you must bear witness also at Rome."*
> Acts 23:11b

Surrounded by enemies who sought his destruction, Paul heard the call of God. Though the man of the Damascus Road had carried the "good news" of Christ to many countries and countless people, the last great labor was to be his best. As Winston Churchill said of the pilots of the Royal Air Force during the Battle for Britain, "This was their finest hour"; so we would describe the last work of Paul as "his finest hour." Though the missionary's witness had been vital in many ways, God had something for him to do that would crown all his previous efforts.

"Take courage," God said, "For as you have testified about me at Jerusalem, so you must bear witness also at Rome." Paul was no longer a young man. Yet it was for this one massive opportunity that he had dreamed and worked so long. God was showing this witness that each moment of life must hold the forward look. At the time when many feel life has lost its real power, God has work for us to do. The difficulties in the latter years are real, but these are the years of the greatest fruitage we have to give. These are the years when the best is yet to come. These are the years that are richest when filled with the forward look.

It is necessary to grasp the understanding that these years are the result of and are a part of natural life-development. We need not be a William Cullen Bryant to discern the message that nature speaks to us in its various moods. The seed is planted in the springtime. It breaks through the earth with blade and shoot until, in full growth, it produces its normal harvest. The trees bloom in the springtime and work all summer till in the fall the ripened fruit is ready to be gathered. The chrysanthemum grows gradually through the long months to garnish the bright days of autumn with gay colors. Paul was not the only one to realize that the greatest opportunities for witness come in the golden days of life. Conrad Adenauer led West Germany when his days numbered more than four score years. Frank Lloyd Wright was planning buildings of amazing architectural design at the age of seventy. Dwight D. Eisenhower served as President of these United States at the age of seventy. The vigor of youth may pass and we may have to husband our strength, but the call to bear witness in Rome is the supreme challenge that comes at the climax of life.

Let us not forget that all the years that went before, the routine of learning and of labor, held only the hint of glory. The blossom of its wondrous beauty is reserved for the mature years. Albert Schweitzer at eighty-five was believed by some to be doing some of his greatest work. Retirement is far from an evil that society has imposed upon us. It is the fulfillment of the years of preparation. Now, for the first time we have the opportunity to make real the hint of glory that has so long burned within us. The dream of Paul to carry the message of Jesus to Rome came when most of us would agree there was little reason to have hope. We, like Paul, are called upon to give our testimony in these latter days.

The best comes last. It does not come by accident but by the purpose of God. Through the years we have mellowed from the brashness of youth to the wisdom of age. We have given up our quest for riches for a nobler quest for full life. We have exchanged our transient purposes for eternal perspectives. It is when the light of life comes upon us. Let us open the corridors of the soul to hear the whisperings of our God, who calls us to "take courage, for as you have testified about me at Jerusalem, so you must bear witness also at Rome."

PRAYER:

Today, O Lord, I realized that the years have fled like dry leaves from the frost-blighted tree. The autumn time is upon me. The hopes and dreams with which I began my witness have found their fulfillment or have been exchanged for better goals. There is a vacant aching in my heart to think that this is all there is. Even as I ponder these things, a strange whispering is in my heart. What! Is there something more for me to do? Lord, lead me gently into the company of Paul and John the "beloved." In these days when the sea of wisdom is full from the streams of experience, let my life bear testimony to thee. Let the labors of my hands, the meditations of my heart, the first of faith within my soul be seen and heard in the counsels of the living. Lord, thou dost give me the upward look. Keep me looking up, keep me moving on, and let my life at least be the best that is in me for thee, through Christ, My Lord. Amen.

IX

In Death and When Hope Is Rekindled

Prepare

Read: Genesis 5:1-5

> *"Thus all the days that Adam lived were nine*
> *hundred and thirty years; and he died."*
> Genesis 5:5

Death is real. From Adam through Christ to each of us, death is a stern reality. Many of us do not come to grips with this fact. Some would join Epicurus who asserted, "When I am, death is not, when death is, I am not; therefore, we can never have anything to do with death." We vaguely hope that by not thinking about it we can escape the inevitability of its reality. The reverse of such an attitude is to contemplate the transition of life to Life with such constancy as to be filled with distilled apprehension. Somewhere between the two positions each of us must discover a solid middle ground; the place wherein we accept the reality of death and embrace a healthy attitude toward that which we move with the speed of passing days.

At the onset we may well recognize that death is a very part of life. When Adnoriam Judson, missionary to Burma, saw his close companion, Wheelock, dying, it became a matter of first importance to prepare his friend for death This was a serious business in which there was much reading of God's Word and sharing of prayers. The dying person was led to give evidence of his confidence about the future life and attendant peace in the face of stern reality. To these people death was a force with which to wrestle and from which victory should emerge. In our gayer times, and as creature comforts make life pleasant here, death is more to be escaped than to be overcome. The middle ground we need for our time is given expression in the language of Russell Dicks, "We must help each person to die with dignity intact." Another way of expressing this is to prepare now for the time when we will face death. And the first thought to pin down is that death is a part of life. About us we see life and death intermingled. The morning heralds the birth day and the shroud of night signals day's death. The sprout emerges from the seed that dies. The flower blossoms only to fade and crumple with the first blight of frost. Even in our family relationships we witness the dying and living that is the normal climate of our days. A son is born into the home. He lives in that home for six years. The day arrives for him to leave the home for his first day in school. A little of the family relationship has died on that day to be replaced with a new relationship that is born. In a sharper sense and with keener emotions, the experience is to come again as the son goes to college and again when he marries. Henry Wadsworth Longfellow understood this matter when he wrote:

> Parting with friends is temporary death,
> As all death is.

Beneath all this living and dying we begin to search for a meaning that will tie life together.

It is here we begin to sense that death is God's gift to us. Adam, in the book of Genesis, is displayed to us that we might see the beginning of things. It is worthy of note that: "Thus all the days that Adam lived were nine hundred and thirty years; and he died." Death was a part of Adam as much as his creation in the image of God. Death belonged to Adam as much as the Garden of Eden, the sweat of his brow, and the years he lived. Death was God's gift to Adam, and thereby, to each of us. It is a precious gift that, like birth, ushers us into a new form of life.

At the other extremity of the Bible we have the witness of our Lord, Jesus Christ to illuminate our lives. Jesus said, "I go to the Father." The inference is that life is eternal. Death, therefore, does not come to change the essential facts of life, but to provide us God's gift to effect the change in the circumstances of life. Lawrence Knowles has put it this way for us:

> When thou, clay cottage, fallest, I'll emerse
> My long-cramp't spirit in the universe.
> Through uncomputed silences of space
> I shall yearn upward to the leaning Face.
> The ancient heavens will roll aside for me,
> As Moses monarch'd the dividing of the sea.
> This body is my house—it is not I.
> Triumphant in this faith I live, and die.[50]

We prepare for death when we see it as a very part of life and as God's gift to effect no change in the nature of life itself, but a change in the circumstances of life.

When we deal with facts, we discover the emergence of newfound courage, strength, and faith. Cancer illuminates this process as do few other diseases. Nonetheless, it is precisely this grasp of reality that each of us needs as we come to grips with death. Ours is not a struggle to overcome, but to do as Jesus said, "But he who endures to the end will be saved" (Mark 13:13). Death is our opportunity to witness to our ability to let God work through us, to witness to our faith in the goodness of God who leads us as a "good Shepherd," to witness to our own dignity of life and assurance of its eternal nature, to witness to our confidence that death is no marauding enemy but a friend—a gift of God.

To prepare ourselves now with such thoughts, to let such thoughts frame our minds and set into confidence, this is to join that grand company that began with Adam and must find part of its continuation in us.

PRAYER:

Lord, keep me from the morbid thought of death. Free me from the dread of pall, shroud, and the narrow opening of earth. Let the old fetters of worn-out ideas drop from my soul. From seeing death as something all strange to life, from seeing it as an end in itself, and for the fault of separating thy presence from death, O Lord, deliver me. Let me see death as a normal part of life. In the confidence with which we accept the dawn of a day and the eventide of time, let me embrace the fact of death. When my heartbeat is strong and steady, when every muscle in my body is keen with life, when new thoughts course through my brain as sunbeams dance upon a dew-kissed meadow, Lord, in such a time let me be preparing for death. So, O God, I would not draw back in stolid fear nor rush with martyr-ardor to answer the meeting with death. But I do want to prepare to meet death with easy confidence and measured tread. Then, as in all circumstances, let the dignity of life capitalize my every thought and enfold me in that grand company of whom Paul said, "We are compassed about by so great a cloud of witnesses." Amen.

The Dark Passage

Read: 1 Corinthians 10:6-13

*"God is faithful, and he will not let you be
tempted beyond your strength . . . that you
may be able to endure it."*
1 Corinthians 10:13b

Fear of dying is often greater than fear of death. With the thought of dying come a thousand swirling questions. Will I bear the strain of suffering? Will my faith be equal to my spiritual needs? Will my mind remain lucid? Will I be able to bear a strong witness to my Christian convictions in the time of change? To these questions we must address ourselves. It is a part of our preparation and a part of our witness to self and others.

The heart of the dark passage centers upon the matter of suffering. For some there is a heightened sense of mental suffering formed by concern over parting from all that seems familiar, safe, secure. Others develop a deep anxiety for the unknown. It is a building of thoughts of "what might happen," and it can lead to a difficult emotional fixation. To not a few, the act of dying holds great dread for physical hurt that frequently manifests itself in malignancies.

The first element of help for these disturbing contemplations is a spiritual understanding of suffering. Paul, in speaking of the human struggle with evil, suggests, "God is faithful, and he will not let you be tempted beyond your strength...that you may be able to endure it." It was Alexis Carrel who appropriated this thought to the level of physical pain. The physician observed that a person can only suffer so much and then no more. The body stands so much pain and then the person faints. As death approaches, the body endures so much hurt only to find relief in coma. God has prepared for our emergencies in the very structure of the body. But there is a larger sense in which we may discover that "God is faithful." The scriptures are filled with assurances of God's attention to our needs. Let us read some of them.

130

So God created man in his own image, in the
image of God he created him; male and female
he created them. And God blessed them....

Genesis 1:27-28a

The LORD is my light and my salvation; whom
shall I fear? The LORD is the stronghold of my life;
of whom shall I be afraid? I believe that I shall see
the goodness of the LORD in the land of the living!
Wait for the LORD; be strong, and let your heart
take courage; yea, wait for the LORD!

Psalm 27:1, 13-14

If you love me, you will keep my commandments.
And I will pray the Father, and he will give you
another Counselor, to be with you for ever, even
the Spirit of truth, whom the world cannot
receive, because it neither sees him nor knows
him; you know him, for he dwells with you, and
will be in you.

John 14:15-16

God has underlaid life with the infinitude of his presence. The
Divine is with us in the times of heartbreak and suffering. The
knowledge that Jesus revealed at his sermon in the upper room
becomes the strength of our assurance, "he dwells with you, and
will be in you."

Again, let us see in our suffering not so much a burden to be
carried as an opportunity to be experienced. Many people live
most of their lives without enduring any prolonged periods of
suffering. A few have spent days and nights enslaved in pain. It
is important for most of us to search out what God would reveal
to us in the sparkling shafts of pain. First, we can discover a new
oneness with God, who knows what it means to suffer through
Jesus Christ on the cross of Calvary. In addition, the individual
learns a sense of patience in which the natural processes of life
cannot be hurried and the inevitable cannot be turned aside. Or,
a new quality of humility can well burst into life. To discover that
the greatest of personal strength or the wonders of science
cannot thwart the merciless development of disease is to realize
a new quality of humility that enlarges the importance of God as

human power diminishes. In a more positive sense, we may well discern new qualities of spiritual maturity through suffering than through any other human experience. Out of the crucible of loss and hurt these words were fashioned on the fifth anniversary of the death of Calvin Coolidge, Jr.:

> You, my son,
> Have shown me God.
>
> . . . .
>
> The memory of your smile, when young,
> Reveals His face,
> As the mellowing years come on apace.[51]

Elizabeth Barrett Browning declares, "Knowledge by suffering entereth..."; and Percy Bysshe Shelley affirms, "They learn in suffering what they teach in song." Hurt and pain may make the body recoil in apprehension, but to the soul seeking to understand God, suffering becomes a solemn teacher of the infinite revelation of a faithful God.

Nor should we go unarmed to face the powers that can hurt the body and unseat the emotions. Strengthened by spiritual insights, it is imperative to understand we never walk this way altogether alone. The physician will be one of our greatest sources of help. Prepared in careful scientific research and the use of medicines, the doctor will seem no less than an angel of mercy. Though no healing comes from her, yet God will work through her to bring healing at its best, or in the last need, to provide release from pain.

There will be the renewing help of the nurses whose kindly voices and gentle hands will express the love that we need. The presence of families will be an added source of strength. Particularly is this true when families use their abilities to lend confidence rather than express concern over the patient's distress. The faces of friends will be an inspiration. They will mean that we are remembered and not forgotten. And let the friends remember that they are showing a new face of remembrance and are not commissioned to impose upon the time or strength of the patient.

We suggest that the minister is a genuine source of help. The minister is named last not because of being least, but because of having the privilege of undergirding the whole experience of suffering with a knowledge of God's Word, through the wonder of prayer that gently leads the mind to eternal assurance, and a warm companionship that allows the patient to flush away doubt and fear through honest conversation.

Suffering must be met with some appreciation that the medical profession is dedicated to the relief of suffering. The use of sedatives and oxygen, together with keeping the body from becoming dehydrated, all form a part of the patient's hope of meeting his needs. Surgery itself is sometimes employed to still the reaction of the nerves of the body to intense pain.

Fear of dying is based upon our fear of suffering. If we are to face suffering with a clear mind and an eager heart, then we shall be prepared for its worst and reveal in our Christian witness the best of our faith. For, in all things, "God is faithful, and he will not let you be tempted beyond your strength...that you may be able to endure it." The best of physician, minister, family, nurses, friends; the best of faith and spiritual insight; the best of all scientific knowledge are joined to express the faithfulness of God to the deepest human needs—even your needs.

PRAYER:

Deliver me, O God, from fears which have no form of personal experience. Give us the hope of hearts that can transpierce the gloom with newfound hope. Reveal to us the reasonableness of suffering as the laborer understands the sweat which bathes the body in grinding toil. Nor let us seek refuge in self-pity which sees disease or accident as a burden which we alone are asked to bear. Let the privilege of pain open the mind to keener thoughts of thee; let the body be consumed that the soul may forebear; let the trials become the training to relinquish our hold on life and find security as thy hand possesses us. Yes, Lord, let the corridor of pain identify us with all persons and with all that you have to give to us. Forgive us for our human impulses which betray our fears. Kindle in us a new faith and hope which constantly witnesses to our assurance that thou art faithful and that thou dost dwell with us and in us, through Jesus Christ our help and peace. Amen.

Escape or Deliverance

Read: 1 Corinthians 15:51-58

*"But thanks be to God, who gives us the
victory through our Lord Jesus Christ."*
1 Corinthians 15:57

The language of our Lord did not allow for the word *escape.*
Jesus had much to say about deliverance. He dwelt firmly upon
the power of faith to provide a new dimension of life. He taught
us to pray, "Lead us not into temptation" (Matthew 6:13a).
When the Master came to the narrow passages of his personal
experiences, the format of escape was not present. Alone on the
mountainside or in a boat on Galilee, Jesus prayed for guidance.
Even in Gethsemane, the words of petition portrayed no spirit of
diverting the will of God nor the inevitable movement of human
affairs. In every moment the Son of God sought the deliverance
of the Eternal, never escape from anything.

Paul, in his personal references, enumerates his difficulties
not to suggest that he sought escape, but that he might magnify
God's work more. Danger attended many of Paul's travels and
death dogged his footsteps. Yet there is no hint that he sought
to evade these difficulties. In much the same manner, as we view
the exigencies of death and suffering, we may find this life of Paul,
the image of Christ's life, as a beginning point for our own lives.

Whether in the vibrancy of health or in the midst of suffering
with death as a reasonable possibility, we may well meditate upon
the following questions:

> Why do I seek the attention of a physician?
> Why do I want to be healed?
> Is God a part of this experience of suffering and
> healing and dying?
> What is the place of my faith in these circum-
> stances?

Am I seeking a means of escape or am I seeking the deliverance of God?

Russell Dicks, widely known counselor and hospital chaplain, would have us believe that "God wills us health." It may be more proper to assert that God wills us good. As a matter of fact, God deals in ultimate purposes first and then with the particulars of life that lead to the ultimate. That is, God wills us good; then, it may well follow that health and suffering both have meaning—even death becomes meaningful—because of the ultimate will of God. All this has much to do with why we seek the attention of a physician.

A doctor recently listed the following reasons patients come to his office: to escape chronic illness and loss of work, to regain health, to escape or overcome suffering, and, in some instances, to prevent death. These all seem legitimate reasons. Yet, each of them, for the most part, deal with the immediate needs of life and are not bound with the ultimates of life or of God. At this point we may well ask, "Why do I want to be healed?" Certainly we may note the following reasons: We wish to retain the security of the present; we do not want to leave the fellowship of loved ones; we wish to share more fully in this earth-existence that we call living. Again, we have answered from the concern of the present, not in relationship to the ultimate. In dealing with the ultimate reason for seeking and protecting health, we need a higher purpose than simply extending the number of our days. However, if we seek to live that we may more fully witness to the power of God in life, then we may have a justifiable reason for living. If this is our justification for seeking health, it may follow that all the other things we wish may be ours because we have first sought to establish our witness to God. The matter of first concern is *why do I seek health?*

We have a life-centered concept of our days. Our definition of life seems to be premised upon the notion that death is a dividing line between life and nothingness. Part of this position is derived from our lack of appreciation for the Christian message on the one hand, and on the other hand an unwillingness to be parted from the abundance that surrounds us. Earth-life, therefore, becomes the cherished goal of human existence. For Christians, this is a denial of the purposes of God as revealed

135

through the resurrection of our Lord, Jesus Christ. Our Creator leaves us with the thought that life is *eternal*, like a thread of time that has neither beginning nor ending. God has created us to form the origin of life and he has given us the risen Christ to establish that neither birth nor death are limitations of real life. Beyond this, God has promised us that his "everlasting arms" will undergird us. In final analysis God upholds us in the midst of every circumstance, and, at last, delivers us into eternal life. God's place in suffering and death is not to show us escape but to show us deliverance from all that can do us real harm.

In the light of such a concept, the faith of each individual becomes a vital force. The formula that Jesus used went something like this: "Your faith has made you whole." Faith is not a force designed to work strange miracles, but to strengthen us in the normal ways of life. Faith opens the canals of the soul for the free movement of God's spirit. Consequently, faith begins with a factual diagnosis of our needs. Until we know what ails us, faith lacks an object. When the diagnosis has been made and confirmed by research, the patient will have a firm foundation for the next step of faith's power, namely to strengthen the patient in the assurance of God's healing process. The fact that the miracle of healing is present as a part of life serves to give us hope. The intricate battle of the human body against disease is the first great element of God's deliverance in which we have faith.

Faith has a great place in our witness through the somber passages of life. It is a faith that combines the power of God with the best that is within us to bring about deliverance from disease and to assure deliverance unto eternal life. When we seek beyond this point, we are on doubtful ground and largely in an area where the human mind cannot understand.

At last, let us remember that Lazarus, who came from the tomb at the call of Christ, finally died. As Christians we are not designed to seek escape, but the deliverance of God to which Paul testified when he said, "But thanks be to God, who gives us the victory through our Lord Jesus Christ."

PRAYER:

Lord of faith, we call thee in the midst of our human needs. From the depths of despair we beseech thee to clear our minds of hidden doubts and fears. Equally, we ask that our minds be freed from dependence upon anticipation of the magical. Stripped of doubt and fear, let faith, ennobled by understanding, become a steadfast hope. Even in the onslaught of pain that will not let us go, may we discipline the soul to find its peace in thee. When we stand face to face with the reality of death, let faith encircle our lives giving us the divine objectives of life. Yes, Lord, we accept thy wondrous gift of "good" for our lives. Still the throbbing doubt that crowds out the good thoughts of thee; quiet our vain human struggle against pain, that we may find the refreshment of thy "still waters"; becalm the quaking distress which overcomes us in the pall of death that we may sense thy resurrection light. In these experiences may our lives bear witness that "nothing can separate us from" thy love which is in Christ Jesus, our Lord, who gives us victory over every ill and all difficulties. These things we pray in the name of him who came to reveal thy goodness to us, even Jesus Christ our Savior. Amen.

Something More

Read: 1 Thessalonians 4:13-18

> " . . . that you may not grieve as others do
> who have no hope."
> 1 Thessalonians 4:13b

In his youth, Voltaire said, "I have to live, and yet I am afraid to die." In latter years he declared, "I die now, loving my friends, not hating my enemies, adoring God and detesting superstition." Between these two remarks stand the years that worked themselves toward maturity of faith. This is the very transition after which all of us seek; it is the wonder of the Christian faith of the pilgrim-pioneer life that blossoms into full witness of that faith.

There is no special time for such growth to begin or to end, yet the necessity for this development is a requisite for our testimony to Christian living. The heart of the matter is that we must come to grips with the reality of death. Myrtle Williamson, in her little book, *One Out of Four,* describes her confrontation with death. She had gone to her doctor for a routine check-up only to discover an emergency operation was needed. Miss Williamson speaks in her own words, "I had to get out of that room. I had to be alone with myself. I had been ready to pay my bill in a doctor's office when suddenly an unspoken word had struck across my mind like a shattering clap of thunder. Like long, continuing peals of thunder, it was now echoing and reechoing through all the places of my being: "Cancer! CANCER!! CANCER!!!"[52]

The first cold wave of shock seems unbearable; then slowly at first, but more surely with time, the power of the Christian witness blossoms into evidence. The first victory in facing death as a reality is related to our overcoming fear. Unfortunately, we have the tradition of the ages to combat. Death has been depicted in the most morbid of characters. The use of the black robe has become a symbol of death. Despite this fact, there is no reason to let such fear control us. The poet Walter Savage Landor gives us this encouraging thought:

> Death stands above me, whispering low
> I know not what into my ear;
> Of his strange language all I know
> Is, there is not a word of fear.[53]

Jesus taught us, "And do not fear those who kill the body but cannot kill the soul" (Matthew 10:28a). Death frequently comes as a friend to give release from prolonged infirmity or protracted illness. The Christian has a much higher assurance. Paul, a prisoner in Rome, wrote these words to Timothy, "The Lord will rescue me from every evil and save me for his heavenly kingdom" (2 Timothy 4:18a). All the great Christians would readily join with Adnariam Judson to declare their joy in reaching the "Golden Shore" to dwell eternally with God. When this great objective fills the soul there is no assurance that fear will not continue, but the means to victory over fear has been established.

Beyond the overcoming of fear stands the assurance that we are not alone in our difficult times. Myrtle Williamson makes clear two of these helps. The first is the awareness of God's power to help us in the deep needs of the soul. Miss Williamson writes, "In spite of my facetiousness, however, ever since the shock of the morning, Paul's testimony to the Romans had been comforting me; surely, if 'nothing can separate us from the love of Christ' *nothing* included cancer, also. And if 'in all these things we are more than conquerors through Christ who loves us,' we can trust God for help; for cancer, it seemed to me, is little more than 'just one of these things.'"[54] The second element of help is what Miss Williamson calls the "covenant community." This is the fellowship of Christ expressed by those with whom we work, live, and worship. The care, love, and prayers of this "covenant community" sustain us and give us strength. The result of these two factors is described by Miss Williamson in these words: "A deep peace that was not of my making" possessed me. "I did not possess it, but it possessed me and filled me with the knowledge that the present moment demanded nothing of me."[55] God provides us the means of overcoming fear and he provides us the "deep peace" to walk in the "valley of the shadow of death."

At last we come to the conviction that death is not the end. Paul observes that we have a *hope* that transforms life. The establishment of this hope is one of the results of our years in the church where we have been taught and where we have worshiped. These have been the years where we made the transition that so vividly marked the life of Voltaire. These are the years that transformed Saul of Tarsus into Paul, "a prisoner of the Lord." These are the years that saw the transition of Jesus as an inquiring lad in the temple at the age of twelve into the man of grand spiritual power as he declared from the cross, "Father, into thy hands I commit my spirit" (Luke 23:46). There is something more to life than living here and now, and there is something more to life than death.

The fullness of our pilgrim-pioneer life as Christians has led us to this one great moment when we give our final witness that God is eternal and there is something more to which we are called.

PRAYER:

Lord, today I came face to face with death. At first I was filled with a fear which caused me to tremble in all my being. My hands shook and my feet were unsteady. The voice of my soul was so distressed that no sound of gladness broke forth. I felt as though all the sure things of life had suddenly been taken away and I was out loose to drift in the awful silence of nothingness.

Into this silence and my blinding fear came thoughts which I did not remember, but they came nonetheless.

"Let not your hearts be troubled; believe in God, believe also in me" (John 14:1).

" And the LORD went before them by day in a pillar of cloud to lead them along the way, and by night in a pillar of fire to give them light..." (Exodus 13:21a).

Slowly at first, then with a mighty rush, I became aware thy spirit was calling to me. Lord, thou art in the midst of death, even as thou art in life itself. Thou art calling me to the fullness of life. Here I have but glimpsed the realities of thy truth. Gently thou art leading me on.

Lord, I cannot say that fear is gone, but the strength of thy presence is greater than my fear. "Lead thou me on," O God, to that which is better. I rest "my weary soul in thee." The throb of pain, the doubt of the future, and the loneliness of the present no longer remain as separate entities. They all merge and are lost as I speed toward thee. Lord, I reach out my heart to thee to accept the best which is yet to come, through Christ my Lord. Amen.

Eternal Witness

Read: 2 Timothy 4:6-8

> *"Henceforth there is laid up for me the*
> *crown of righteousness . . . ."*
> 2 Timothy 4:8a

The Lebanese mystic Kahlil Gibran once wrote:

> I shall live beyond death, and
> I shall sing in your ears
> Even after the vast sea-wave
> carries me back
> To the vast sea-depth.

> I shall sit at your board though
> without a body,
> And I shall go with you to your
> fields, a spirit invisible.
> I shall come to you at your
> fireside, a guest unseen.
> Death changes nothing but the
> masks that cover our faces.

> The woodsman shall be still a woodsman,
> The ploughman, a ploughman.
> And he who gave his song to the wind
> shall sing it also to the moving spheres.[56]

What the mystic discovered in meditative contemplation, the scientist has achieved in the realm of reason. Dr. Harold C. DeWindt has this to say to us: "Science says nothing in this world can be destroyed. You burn a log in your fireplace, and it is gone as a log, but not one constitutional element of it has been lost. Would a wise Creator preserve the lowest elements and let the highest perish? The greatest thinkers believed in immortality because if there were no other world than this life, then life is a farce. If there is no beyond where wrongs are righted and justice is meted out, then life is but a shadow dance."[57] "Death changes nothing but the masks that cover our faces," and there is a touch of immortality in all things mortal. To these convictions of the mystic and of the scientist, Paul adds another element. It is the dimension of eternal witness. As Paul wrote to Timothy, there comes the irresistable urge to declare this conviction, "Henceforth there is laid up for me the crown of righteousness." Paul had done many things, but never had he worn a crown. Now, in the deepest expression of faith, this disciple of our Lord asserts that we will come to the time when we shall wear a "crown of righteousness." In the imagery of our Lord, it is like being called from the foot of the table to become a part of the honored guests at the head of the table. The years of Paul's ministry had been filled with persecution and trouble, now the future becomes gloriously bright. Paul did not see his ministry ended, but extended. For so long, he had been ministering to those among whom he walked and taught. The time was coming when he would become a part of that great cloud of witnesses that "encompasses" us all. Then, the new ministry would call him to continue to bear testimony to God.

We began these meditations with the theme that God chooses us. The promise of immortality is God's final choosing of us. Our work is not concluded, it simply has a new locus of operation. Our message may not be essentially changed, but divinely refined. And our companionship, while broken in part, finds a new unison in the oneness of God through Jesus Christ. As pilgrims we have sought the leading of the spirit of the eternal. As pioneers we have courageously sought to give God our best in the normal experiences of life. In every circumstance, we have sought to find the genius of bearing our witness of Christian faith. Finally, we are lifted to the supreme level of eternal witness. All we have learned and experienced, we now will express on a higher level. The writer of 1 John leads our thoughts in this way: "That which we have seen and heard we proclaim also to you, so that you may have fellowship with us; and our fellowship is with the Father and with his Son Jesus Christ" (1 John 1:3).

God has chosen us to proclaim God's truth upon this earth and to bear an eternal witness. The testimony of our days has prepared us, by God's grace, for this nobler task. The task to which we are called may have various conditions, but the task itself cannot be different. As we are expected to give evidence of God's love here and now, so we must continue so to do as we partake in the "crown of righteousness." John Oxenham gives us a triumphant view when he writes:

> There is no death,
> They only truly live
> Who pass into the land beyond,
> And see
> This earth is but a school of preparation
> For a larger ministry.[58]

Out of the complex of our days filled with choosing, toil, defeat, pain, and death emerges the final victory of the pilgrim-pioneer. It is the victory of a witness sought and achieved in part to be fulfilled in the eternal witness amid the fellowship of those who, like ourselves, have received from God the "crown of righteousness."

PRAYER:

O God, thou hast rekindled hope within my life. At first thou didst speak to me in accents uncertain because my self-will crowded out the syllable of thy love. As the years of life piled high, my strength was unequal to my tasks, and thy voice became more clear. In the midst of heartache, disappointment, and pain thou hast become ever dearer to me. Now it seems that all the bright promises earth-life offered have paled with time, and all thy promises of eternal life have become real. My heart swells with raptured gratitude for thy leading spirit, even when I turned from thee or did not sense thy leading. I know my struggles are not over and failure will confront me again, but I now know that thou wilt never forsake me.

O Lord, receive the anthems of my praise for the wonder of the pilgrim-pioneer way of life. Accept, I beseech thee, the feeble witness of my often faltering faith. By thy grace, forgive my sins and, at last, give me thy peace which "passeth understanding." I do not ask for regal attire nor for places of honor. Let it be enough that I may share thy "crown of righteousness" where hope forever shatters fear and where love overcomes life's problems, and where faith will make me constant in my witness to thee. This I humbly pray in Christ, who strengthens me, even my Lord. Amen.

Notes

[1]James Dalton Morrison, editor, *Masterpieces of Religious Verse.* Harper & Brothers, 1948, p. 353-354.

[2]Daniel Jenkins, *The Strangeness of the Church.* Doubleday and Co., Inc., 1955, p. 10.

[3]George Santayana, *The Idea of Christ in the Gospels.* Scribners, 1946, p. 192.

[4]Thomas Dunn English, "Keep the Mill a-Going."

[5]Emil Brunner, *Christianity and Civilization.* Charles Scribner's Sons, 1949, p. 35.

[6]C.E. Rounsefell, *"I'll Go Where You Want Me to Go."* Homer Rodeheaver, Owner, 1922.

[7]Robert Frost, "The Gift Outright" from *A Witness Tree.* Henry Holt & Company, 1942.

[8]Phillip Doddridge and John Logan, "O God of Bethel, by Whose Hand."

[9]Whitaker Chambers, *Witness.* Random House, 1952.

[10]Basil Miller, *Ten Handicapped People Who Became Famous.* Zondervan Publishing House, 1951, p. 43.

[11]Robert Southey, "The Curse of Kehama." Canto X, Stanza 10.

[12]Henry Drummond, *The Greatest Thing in the World.* London Book Co., Inc., n.d., pp. 11-12.

[13]Robert Browning, "Apollo and the Fates," Stanza 42.

[14]Anne Morrow Lindbergh, "Two Citadels" from *The Unicorn.* Pantheon Press, 1956.

[15]Hillyer Straton, *Solving Life's Problems.* The Bethany Press,1954, p. 28.

[16]Pearl S. Buck, *My Several Worlds.* John Day, 1954, p.51.

[17]Straton, *Solving Life's Problems,* pp. 17-18.

[18]Rudyard Kipling, "If" from *Rewards and Fairies.* (Copyright by Rudyard Kipling, 1910.)

[19]Paul Elmen, *The Restoration of Meaning to Contemporary Life.* Doubleday, 1958, p. 151.

[20]William Shakespeare, *Othello.*

[21]William Henry Davies, "Hunting Joy."

[22]*Interpreter's Bible*, Volume 10, p. 566.

[23]Fulton Oursler, *Modern Parables.* Doubleday, 1950, pp. 30ff.

[24]John Milton, "On His Blindness."

[25]Elinor Wylie, "Calvary."

[26]Harold Wilke, *Strengthened with Might.* The Westminster Press, 1952, p. 74.

[27]Clifford Bax, "The Musician."

[28]Helmut Thielicke, *The Waiting Father*. Harper & Brothers, 1959, p. 23.

[29]K.R. Eissler, *The Psychiatrist and the Dying Patient*. International Universities Press, Inc., 1955, p. 46.

[30]Alice Duer Miller, *The White Cliffs*. Coward-McCann, Inc., 1940, p. 49.

[31]Eissler, *The Psychiatrist and the Dying Patient*, p. 167.

[32]Terry E. Lilly, Jr., M.D., Kansas City, Missouri.

[33]William Shakespeare, *Julius Caesar*.

[34]Eissler, *The Psychiatrist and the Dying Patient*, p. 115.

[35]Henry Cuyler Bunner, "The Wail of the Personally Conducted," Stanza 6.

[36]Oliver Goldsmith, "The Vicar of Wakefield," Chapter 5, Song, Stanza 1.

[37]Rudyard Kipling, "The Last of the Light Brigade," Stanza 8.

[38]Wayne E. Oates, *Religious Factors in Mental Illness*. Association Press, 1955, p. 172.

[39]A.H. Maslow and Bela Mittlemann, *Principles of Abnormal Psychology*. Harper & Brothers.

[40]*Thoughts of Saint Therese*. P.J. Kenedy & Sons, 1915, p. 23.

[41]A.C. Swinburne, "A Sea-Mark," Stanza 5.

[42]George Eliot, "The Tide of Faith."

[43]Richard Burton, "Strength in Weakness."

[44]Quoted in William Oursler, *The Healing Power of Faith*. Hawthorne Books, Inc., 1957, p. 159.

[45]*The Christian-Evangelist*, St. Louis, November 22, 1950.

[46]*St. Louis Globe-Democrat*, May 21, 1957.

[47]Samuel Smiles, "Life and Labor."

[48]William G. Tarrant, "My Master Was a Worker."

[49]Elton Trueblood, *The Common Ventures of Life*. Harper & Brothers, 1949, p. 103.

[50]Lawrence Knowles, "The Tenant."

[51]Grace Coolidge, "The Open Door."

[52]Myrtle Williamson, *One Out of Four*. John Knox Press, 1960, p. 14.

[53]Walter Savage Landor, "Death Stands Above Me."

[54]*Ibid.*, p. 26.

[55]*Ibid.*, p. 30.

[56]Kahlil Gibran, *The Garden of the Prophet*. Alfred A. Knopf, Inc., 1933, pp. 61ff.

[57]Harold C. DeWindt, "Why I Believe in Life After Death." *Farm Journal*, April 1959.

[58]John Oxenham, "The Vision Splendid."